I0009444

Table Of Contents

Section 7: Case Studies and Real-World Examples

Section 8: Troubleshooting and Optimization

Section 9: The Future and Final Tips

Appendices

- Appendix A: Keyboard Shortcuts Cheat Sheet
- Appendix B: Template Library for Complex Projects
- Appendix C: Glossary of ClickUp Terminology
- Appendix D: Resources for Continued Learning

~ Conclusion

Disclaimer

This book is an independent resource and is not officially affiliated with, endorsed by, or sponsored by any company, organization, or trademark holder referenced within. All trademarks, service marks, product names, and company names or logos mentioned are the property of their respective owners. Use of these names or terms is solely for identification and reference purposes, and no association or endorsement by the respective trademark holder is implied. The content of this book is based on publicly available information, the author's research, and personal insights. This book is intended for educational and informational purposes only.

Welcome & What You'll Learn

Welcome to *ClickUp for Complex Projects*

Managing complex projects is no small feat. Whether you're leading a fast-paced software development team, overseeing large-scale marketing campaigns, or handling intricate healthcare operations, the challenge remains the same—keeping everything organized, ensuring clear communication, and driving efficiency without losing sight of critical details.

This book is designed to help you harness the full power of **ClickUp**, a highly versatile project management tool, to streamline your workflow, enhance team productivity, and successfully navigate the complexities of modern project management.

Why This Book?

Many professionals struggle to implement an effective project management system, especially when dealing with multifaceted projects that involve multiple stakeholders, shifting priorities, and interdependent tasks. ClickUp offers a robust set of tools, but unlocking its full potential requires a strategic approach.

This book provides a **detailed, step-by-step guide** on setting up, optimizing, and mastering ClickUp for **complex projects**. Whether you're new to ClickUp or already familiar with its features, you'll gain **insights, best practices, and advanced techniques** that will help you elevate your project management game.

What You'll Learn

By the time you finish this book, you will:

■ **Understand Complex Project Management Challenges** – Learn about the key difficulties project managers face and how ClickUp can provide tailored solutions.

■ **Master ClickUp's Core Features** – Gain hands-on knowledge of how to structure your **workspaces, spaces, folders, lists, and tasks** efficiently.

■ **Optimize Workflows for Scalability** – Discover strategies for setting up custom views, automations, custom fields, and reporting dashboards to **reduce manual effort** and boost productivity.

■ **Enhance Team Collaboration** – Learn how to assign tasks effectively, leverage ClickUp Docs for centralized documentation, and use communication tools like comments, chat, and mentions to keep teams aligned.

■ **Implement Advanced Techniques for Complex Workflows** – Dive into ClickUp's most powerful capabilities, including **dependencies, multi-location tasks, integrations, and goal tracking**, to manage sophisticated project structures.

■ **Solve Common Challenges and Optimize Performance** – Address **common errors, performance bottlenecks, and troubleshooting methods** to ensure ClickUp runs smoothly, even as your projects scale.

Who This Book Is For

This book is ideal for:

- **Project Managers** handling multi-phase, cross-functional projects.
- **Team Leads & Executives** looking to enhance productivity and visibility.

- **Agile & Scrum Practitioners** managing sprints and iterative workflows.
- **Operations Managers** coordinating complex business processes.
- **Freelancers & Consultants** who need a flexible, scalable project management system.

No matter your industry or role, if you manage projects that involve multiple moving parts, ClickUp can become your **ultimate project management ally**—and this book will show you exactly how to leverage it to its fullest potential.

How This Book Is Structured

This book is divided into **nine sections**, guiding you from the **fundamentals of ClickUp** to its **most advanced capabilities**:

📌 **Section 1: Introduction to ClickUp and Complex Projects** – Gain a solid foundation in complex project management and why ClickUp is a game-changer.

📌 **Section 2: Setting Up ClickUp for Success** – Learn the best way to structure your ClickUp **hierarchy, views, and data imports** for maximum efficiency.

📌 **Section 3: Core Features for Project Management** – Master essential features like **task management, automations, custom fields, and tracking progress**.

📌 **Section 4: Advanced Techniques for Complexity** – Take your ClickUp expertise further with **dependencies, multi-location tasks, dashboards, and advanced reporting**.

📌 **Section 5: Collaboration and Team Productivity** – Optimize teamwork through **comments, roles, permissions, and real-time communication**.

📌 **Section 6: Integrations and Extensions** – Learn how to **connect ClickUp** with other essential tools like Slack, Google Drive, and Zoom for a seamless workflow.

📌 **Section 7: Case Studies and Real-World Examples** – See **how different industries** use ClickUp to manage projects efficiently.

📌 **Section 8: Troubleshooting and Optimization** – Address common **ClickUp challenges, optimize performance, and stay updated with new features**.

📌 **Section 9: The Future and Final Tips** – Explore the **future of ClickUp** and how to sustain long-term productivity gains.

Final Thoughts

ClickUp is more than just a task management tool—it's a **powerful platform that can transform the way you work**. However, simply having access to great software isn't enough; knowing how to set it up, configure it for your needs, and use it effectively makes all the difference.

Through this book, you'll gain **the skills, strategies, and confidence** to master ClickUp for complex projects and drive **exceptional team productivity and efficiency**.

Let's dive in! 🚀

Section 1:
Introduction to ClickUp and Complex Projects

Understanding Complex Project Management Challenges

Project management, in any form, is a balancing act between **planning, execution, resource management, and communication**. However, **complex projects** introduce additional layers of intricacy, often involving:

- **Multiple teams and stakeholders** with varying priorities
- **Interdependent tasks** that must align seamlessly
- **Frequent scope changes** due to evolving business needs
- **Strict deadlines and budget constraints**
- **Data-driven decision-making** requiring real-time insights

A project becomes **complex** when it extends beyond simple task tracking and requires a structured approach to handle dependencies, uncertainties, and high coordination demands.

Key Challenges in Complex Project Management

Managing large-scale, intricate projects presents several difficulties. Let's break down the most common challenges and their impact on teams and organizations.

1 Managing Multiple Workstreams Simultaneously

In a complex project, different teams may be working on different **workstreams** that must eventually come together. Coordinating efforts across these teams without creating bottlenecks is a significant challenge.

Example:

A **software development team** might be working on backend development while the frontend team is designing the user interface. Both must align to ensure compatibility, requiring detailed tracking and coordination.

Impact:

Without a centralized system, communication gaps arise, leading to **delays, inefficiencies, and misaligned expectations**.

2 Tracking Dependencies and Interconnected Tasks

Unlike simple projects where tasks are mostly independent, complex projects often have **dependencies**—tasks that cannot start until others are completed.

Example:

A **marketing campaign launch** may depend on:
- The completion of branding assets
- Approval of messaging from stakeholders
- Technical setup for ads and landing pages

Impact:

Without clear dependency tracking, teams may work on **misaligned priorities**, resulting in delays and last-minute rushes.

③ Handling Frequent Scope Changes

Complex projects rarely follow a linear path. **Stakeholder demands, market shifts, or unforeseen risks** often require scope adjustments.

Example:

A **product development project** may need to add new features mid-way due to competitor advancements.

Impact:

Without a **flexible project management system**, sudden scope changes can cause **resource strain, missed deadlines, and team frustration**.

④ Ensuring Effective Cross-Team Collaboration

When multiple teams, departments, or even external vendors are involved, collaboration challenges emerge. Information silos, lack of shared context, and miscommunication can **derail** project progress.

Example:

In an **enterprise-wide software rollout**, IT, HR, and finance teams must collaborate, but each has different priorities and workflows.

Impact:

Disjointed collaboration leads to **misaligned goals, duplicated work, and slower decision-making**.

⑤ Managing Resource Allocation Efficiently

Resource allocation in complex projects requires balancing **team availability, budget constraints, and workload distribution**. Overloaded teams lead to burnout, while underutilized teams cause inefficiency.

Example:

A **video production company** must allocate designers, editors, and scriptwriters effectively to avoid bottlenecks.

Impact:

Poor resource management results in **delayed deliveries, overworked employees, and unnecessary costs**.

⑥ Ensuring Visibility and Real-Time Progress Tracking

Complex projects involve multiple moving parts. Stakeholders, from executives to team members, need **real-time insights** on progress, risks, and blockers.

Example:

A **construction project manager** needs real-time data on **material procurement, task completion, and workforce availability**.

Impact:

Without proper visibility, teams struggle to **identify risks early, measure performance, and make data-driven decisions**.

7 Automating Repetitive Processes to Reduce Workload

Manual updates, redundant communication, and repetitive approvals slow down projects. Automating workflows can free up time for **high-value tasks**.

Example:

A **customer support team** could automate ticket assignments based on urgency and expertise, reducing response times.

Impact:

Without automation, teams waste **hours on manual updates**, leading to inefficiencies and missed opportunities for optimization.

How ClickUp Addresses These Challenges

ClickUp is uniquely designed to tackle these challenges through its **highly customizable features** that allow teams to build workflows suited to their specific needs.

Here's how ClickUp helps overcome common complex project challenges:

■ **Multiple Workstreams? Use Workspaces, Spaces, and Folders** to separate different projects while maintaining cross-team visibility.

■ **Managing Dependencies? ClickUp's Task Relationships and Gantt Charts** help visualize dependencies clearly.

■ **Frequent Scope Changes? Custom Fields and Agile Boards** allow for flexibility in adjusting priorities without losing track of original goals.

■ **Cross-Team Collaboration? ClickUp Docs, Comments, and Mentions** enable seamless communication across teams.

■ **Resource Allocation? Time Tracking and Workload Views** help distribute tasks efficiently without overloading team members.

■ **Real-Time Tracking? Dashboards, Reports, and Milestone Tracking** provide up-to-date project insights.

■ **Reducing Manual Work? ClickUp Automations** streamline repetitive tasks and improve efficiency.

The Need for a Strategic Approach

While ClickUp offers the tools to address these challenges, **understanding how to configure and use them effectively** is crucial.

That's what this book will teach you—**a detailed, structured approach** to using ClickUp for **managing complex projects** efficiently.

In the next chapters, we'll dive deeper into:

📌 **Why ClickUp is the Best Tool for Complex Projects** (Chapter 2)
📌 **How to Structure Your ClickUp Workspace for Maximum Efficiency** (Chapter 4)
📌 **Best Practices for Automations, Dependencies, and Reporting** (Chapters 11-19)

By the end of this book, you'll have a **comprehensive strategy** for making ClickUp work for your **most demanding projects**.

Why ClickUp Stands Out for Complex Workflows

Managing complex projects requires a tool that goes beyond basic task tracking. As teams become more distributed, projects more intricate, and workflows more dynamic, traditional project management software often falls short. **ClickUp stands out as one of the most versatile, scalable, and customizable platforms available, making it an ideal choice for handling complex workflows.**

But what makes ClickUp different from other project management tools? Why is it particularly well-suited for complex projects? This chapter explores the key reasons why ClickUp is a game-changer for teams managing intricate, multi-layered workflows.

What Makes ClickUp Unique?

Unlike many project management tools that focus on a single methodology (e.g., Agile, Kanban, or Waterfall), **ClickUp is designed to be highly adaptable**, accommodating diverse teams and their unique needs.

Here's why ClickUp is the **go-to solution for complex workflows**:

1 A Flexible Hierarchy for Organizing Complex Projects

One of ClickUp's biggest strengths is its **hierarchical structure**, which allows teams to **break down complex projects into manageable components**.

📌 **Key Structural Elements in ClickUp:**

- **Workspaces** → The highest level, ideal for large organizations or departments
- **Spaces** → Separate areas within a Workspace for different teams or initiatives
- **Folders** → Used to categorize related projects within a Space
- **Lists** → Collections of tasks within a Folder, allowing for structured planning
- **Tasks & Subtasks** → The building blocks of project execution, supporting dependencies and detailed breakdowns

🛠 **Why It Matters for Complex Projects:**
Traditional project management tools often struggle with multi-tiered projects, forcing teams into rigid structures. ClickUp's **nested hierarchy ensures that large projects remain well-organized and scalable**, accommodating teams of all sizes.

2 Customizable Views for Different Teams and Workflows

Complex projects involve different stakeholders—executives, managers, designers, engineers, and marketers—each needing different **ways to visualize progress**.

📌 **ClickUp's View Options Include:**
■ **List View** – Ideal for detailed task breakdowns
■ **Board View (Kanban)** – Great for Agile workflows and visual task tracking
■ **Gantt Charts** – Essential for timeline planning and managing dependencies
■ **Calendar View** – Perfect for deadline-driven projects
■ **Dashboard View** – Provides high-level insights for executives and decision-makers

🛠 **Why It Matters for Complex Projects:**
Traditional tools often lock teams into **one rigid view**, but ClickUp allows everyone to **customize their experience**, ensuring visibility **without disrupting workflows**.

3 Advanced Task Management Features

A robust task management system is critical for **breaking down large projects into manageable parts**. ClickUp excels in this area with features that enhance **organization, collaboration, and efficiency**.

📌 **ClickUp's Key Task Management Features:**

- **Task Dependencies** → Ensure tasks follow a logical sequence
- **Multi-Location Tasks** → Assign tasks across multiple Lists/Projects
- **Recurring Tasks** → Automate repetitive processes
- **Checklists & Subtasks** → Provide deeper task granularity
- **Priority Levels & Statuses** → Track critical vs. non-critical tasks

🛠 **Why It Matters for Complex Projects:**
Many project management tools lack **true task interconnectivity**, forcing teams to use separate tools for tracking dependencies. ClickUp **natively supports** complex workflows, reducing reliance on external integrations.

4 Automations to Reduce Manual Work

Managing complex projects often involves **repetitive administrative work** that can slow down teams. ClickUp's **Automations** allow users to **eliminate manual processes** and **enhance efficiency**.

📌 **Automation Capabilities Include:**
- Auto-assigning tasks based on specific conditions
- Updating statuses when task criteria are met
- Triggering notifications or Slack messages when deadlines approach
- Creating recurring tasks without manual setup

🛠 **Why It Matters for Complex Projects:**
Large-scale projects require **speed and efficiency**. ClickUp's Automations allow teams to **focus on strategic work instead of manual updates**, saving time and reducing errors.

5 Real-Time Collaboration and Documentation

One of ClickUp's standout features is its built-in **collaboration tools**, which help teams **stay aligned without switching between multiple platforms**.

📌 **Key Collaboration Features:**

- **Docs & Wikis** → Centralized documentation within projects
- **Comments & Mentions** → Instant feedback and discussions on tasks
- **ClickUp Chat** → Internal messaging without needing Slack or email
- **Shared Whiteboards** → Visual brainstorming for project planning

🛠 **Why It Matters for Complex Projects:**
Many teams rely on **disjointed tools** like Google Docs, Slack, and Notion for collaboration. ClickUp **consolidates these features into one platform**, making communication more efficient.

6 Custom Dashboards for Real-Time Insights

In complex projects, **stakeholders need quick access to critical metrics**. ClickUp's Dashboards offer **customizable widgets** for tracking **team progress, workload distribution, goal completion, and more**.

📌 **Dashboard Widgets Include:**
- Task Progress Trackers
- Workload Distribution Charts
- Time Tracking Reports
- Custom Goal Tracking

⚒ Why It Matters for Complex Projects:
Instead of manually compiling reports, teams can **automate performance tracking**, giving decision-makers **instant access to the data they need**.

7 Powerful Integrations and API Access

Most complex projects involve **multiple tools**, from CRM systems to development platforms. ClickUp integrates with **over 1,000 apps**, allowing teams to connect their workflows effortlessly.

📌 Popular Integrations Include:
- Slack & Microsoft Teams – For real-time communication
- Google Drive & Dropbox – For file sharing
- Jira & GitHub – For development teams
- Zoom – For virtual meetings
- Custom API Access – For building tailored solutions

⚒ Why It Matters for Complex Projects:
Rather than juggling **multiple disconnected tools**, ClickUp's **seamless integrations** create a unified project ecosystem, reducing friction and improving productivity.

Why ClickUp Is the Right Choice for Complex Workflows

ClickUp's all-in-one approach eliminates the need for multiple project management tools, **simplifying workflows while increasing efficiency**. Whether you're handling **product development, marketing campaigns, enterprise operations, or cross-functional initiatives**, ClickUp provides:

- **Unmatched flexibility** for structuring projects
- **Multiple visualization options** to accommodate different teams
- **Powerful task management** with dependencies and automation
- **Seamless collaboration features** for teams of all sizes
- **Real-time dashboards** for data-driven decision-making
- **Robust integrations** for a streamlined tech stack

Let's dive deeper into how this book is structured.

Overview of the Book's Structure and Goals

Project management has evolved significantly in recent years, and tools like **ClickUp** have revolutionized the way teams handle complex projects. However, simply having access to ClickUp isn't enough—it's how you **set it up, optimize it, and align it with your workflows** that determines success.

This book is designed to be **your comprehensive guide to mastering ClickUp for complex projects**. Whether you're a project manager, team lead, executive, or freelancer handling high-stakes work, this book will help you build **scalable, efficient, and highly productive** workflows using ClickUp.

How This Book is Structured

To ensure that you gain **a deep and actionable understanding of ClickUp**, this book is divided into **nine structured sections**, each focusing on a different aspect of using ClickUp for complex project management.

📌 Section 1: Introduction to ClickUp and Complex Projects

Before diving into ClickUp's features, it's important to **understand the core challenges of complex project management**. This section introduces:

- The difficulties teams face when managing large-scale projects
- Why ClickUp is uniquely suited to handle these challenges
- A roadmap of what you will learn in this book

By the end of this section, you will have a **clear perspective on how ClickUp can serve as a powerful solution** for your project management needs.

📌 Section 2: Setting Up ClickUp for Success

ClickUp's effectiveness depends on **how well it is structured**. This section provides a **step-by-step guide to setting up ClickUp** for optimal efficiency. Topics include:

- Establishing **Workspaces, Spaces, Folders, and Lists**
- Structuring ClickUp to **scale with your organization**
- Customizing views to match different **project types and work styles**
- Importing existing data and migrating from other tools

By the end of this section, you'll have **a well-organized ClickUp environment** tailored to your needs.

📌 Section 3: Core Features for Project Management

This section covers the **most critical ClickUp features** that teams use daily, including:

- Task Management & Breaking Down Complex Deliverables
- Docs for Centralized Knowledge Management
- Gantt Charts & Timelines for Long-Term Planning
- Automations to Reduce Manual Workload
- Custom Fields for Tailored Workflows
- Prioritization and Status Tracking

Mastering these features will help you **build a structured yet flexible workflow** that keeps your projects moving forward efficiently.

📌 Section 4: Advanced Techniques for Complexity

As projects grow in size and complexity, standard task management isn't enough. This section explores **advanced techniques** to enhance productivity and ensure seamless execution, including:

- Managing Dependencies & Subtasks for intricate workflows
- Multi-Location Tasks for cross-team collaboration
- Creating Custom Dashboards for real-time insights
- Time Tracking & Resource Allocation for efficient workload balancing
- Aligning Goals with Project Milestones
- Advanced Reporting for Stakeholder Communication

By implementing these advanced techniques, you'll **optimize ClickUp for large-scale, high-impact projects**.

📌 Section 5: Collaboration and Team Productivity

ClickUp is **not just a task manager—it's a collaboration powerhouse**. This section explores **how to maximize teamwork using ClickUp's built-in communication tools**, including:

- Real-Time Collaboration using Comments and Mentions
- Strategic Role & Permission Assignments
- Using ClickUp Chat for Seamless Communication
- Establishing Feedback Loops & Iterative Workflows

By the end of this section, your team will have **a structured communication process**, ensuring that information flows efficiently across all members.

📌 Section 6: Integrations and Extensions

ClickUp's power extends beyond its native features. This section will show you how to **enhance your ClickUp experience** by integrating it with other essential tools:

- Connecting ClickUp with **Slack, Google Drive, Zoom, and other platforms**
- Leveraging the **ClickUp API for custom solutions**
- Using **browser extensions** for faster task management

These integrations will help you create **a seamless, end-to-end project management ecosystem**.

📌 Section 7: Case Studies and Real-World Examples

Theory is great, but **real-world application is even better**. This section provides **detailed case studies** demonstrating how different industries and teams use ClickUp to **solve real challenges**:

- **Tech Startup:** Managing Agile Sprints
- **Marketing Agency:** Coordinating Multi-Client Campaigns
- **Healthcare Project:** Tracking Compliance & Patient Care Tasks
- **Remote Teams:** Ensuring Global Workflow Synchronization

By studying these real-life use cases, you'll gain **practical insights and best practices** to implement in your own work.

📌 Section 8: Troubleshooting and Optimization

ClickUp is a powerful tool, but **like any software, it requires fine-tuning**. This section covers **common pitfalls and performance optimizations**, including:

- Resolving **common errors and technical issues**
- Optimizing ClickUp for **speed and performance**
- Staying updated with **new features and best practices**

By the end of this section, you'll be able to **resolve issues quickly and ensure your ClickUp setup remains efficient over time**.

📌 **Section 9: The Future and Final Tips**

ClickUp is continuously evolving. This final section explores:

- The **future of ClickUp** and upcoming trends in project management
- Final productivity strategies to **ensure long-term efficiency**
- Tips for **sustaining project management excellence**

What You'll Achieve by Reading This Book

By the time you finish *ClickUp for Complex Projects*, you will:

■ **Understand how to structure ClickUp for maximum efficiency**
■ **Master core and advanced ClickUp features to manage complex projects**
■ **Learn best practices for team collaboration and automation**
■ **Discover how to integrate ClickUp with other essential tools**
■ **Gain insights from real-world case studies and examples**
■ **Know how to troubleshoot and optimize ClickUp for long-term success**

How to Use This Book

📌 **For Beginners** → If you are new to ClickUp, start with **Section 2** to build a strong foundation.
📌 **For Intermediate Users** → If you're already familiar with ClickUp, focus on **Sections 3 and 4** to unlock advanced features.
📌 **For Experts** → If you're managing enterprise-level projects, **Sections 5, 6, and 7** will help you scale operations and streamline collaboration.

No matter where you are in your project management journey, this book provides **actionable guidance and proven strategies** to take your ClickUp usage to the next level.

Moving Forward

Now that you understand the book's structure and what you'll gain, it's time to **dive into the practical aspects of using ClickUp for complex workflows**.

Section 2:
Setting Up ClickUp for Success

Initial Setup: Workspaces, Spaces, and Folders

ClickUp's **true power lies in its flexibility**, allowing you to create a structure that suits your specific needs. However, without a **clear setup strategy**, teams can quickly become overwhelmed, leading to **disorganized projects, unclear task assignments, and inefficient workflows**.

This chapter will walk you through the **essential first steps** to setting up ClickUp correctly by understanding and leveraging:
■ **Workspaces** – The foundation of your ClickUp environment
■ **Spaces** – Distinct project areas within your workspace
■ **Folders** – Groupings of related projects and tasks

By the end of this chapter, you will have a **well-structured ClickUp account** tailored for complex project management.

📌 Step 1: Creating and Configuring Your ClickUp Workspace

What is a Workspace?

A **Workspace** is the highest-level container in ClickUp, acting as the **main hub** where all your teams, projects, and tasks reside. Think of it as the **"company-wide headquarters"** for all your work.

Best Practices for Setting Up Your Workspace

[1] **Create a New Workspace**

- If you are new to ClickUp, create a **new workspace** by signing up and selecting **"Create Workspace"** from the settings.
- If your organization already has a ClickUp workspace, request access if necessary.

[2] **Name Your Workspace Clearly**

- Use a **clear and identifiable name** to avoid confusion.
- Examples:
  ■ *Acme Corp Project Management*
  ■ *Tech Startup Ops*
  ■ *Marketing Agency HQ*

[3] **Set Up General Workspace Settings**

- Under **"Settings"**, configure **time zones, currency formats, and default priorities**.
- Adjust **notifications and permissions** to align with your organization's workflow.

[4] **Invite Team Members**

- Go to **"People"** and invite relevant team members.
- Assign appropriate **permissions** to ensure data security and role clarity.

📌 Step 2: Structuring Your Spaces for Better Organization

What is a Space?

Spaces act as **separate divisions** within a workspace, allowing teams or departments to organize work independently. Think of them as **major work categories or teams** within your organization.

How to Use Spaces Effectively

📌 **Examples of Space Structures:**
■ *Department-Based Spaces* – Best for larger organizations

- Marketing
- Product Development
- HR & Operations
- Sales & Customer Support

■ *Project-Based Spaces* – Best for agencies and consulting firms

- Client A – Website Development
- Client B – Digital Marketing
- Client C – IT Infrastructure

■ *Workflow-Based Spaces* – Ideal for Agile teams

- Sprint Backlog
- Active Projects
- Completed Projects

Best Practices:
✔ **Keep Spaces Organized** – Avoid unnecessary Spaces; use **Folders and Lists** for detailed structuring.
✔ **Assign Owners** – Each Space should have a **clear owner or admin** responsible for managing its setup.
✔ **Customize Space Settings** – Enable or disable **features like Goals, Automations, and Docs** based on the needs of the team.

📌 Step 3: Using Folders to Group Related Projects

What is a Folder?

Folders are **containers within Spaces** that help **group related Lists together**, making them ideal for organizing multiple projects or task categories under a single umbrella.

How to Use Folders Effectively

📌 **Folder Examples:**
■ **For a Tech Startup Space:**

- *Product Development* (Features, Bug Fixes, Testing)
- *Operations* (Recruitment, HR, Legal)
- *Marketing Campaigns* (SEO, Content Strategy, Paid Ads)

■ **For a Marketing Agency Space:**

- *Client A – Campaigns*
- *Client B – Social Media*
- *Client C – Branding Projects*

Best Practices:
✔ **Use Folders for Multi-Phase Projects** – If a project has multiple steps, create **dedicated Folders** for each phase.
✔ **Avoid Overcomplicating** – If your team prefers simplicity, **use Lists instead of Folders** for task grouping.
✔ **Enable Folder-Specific Views** – Customize **Gantt, Board, or Calendar views** based on the workflow needs.

📌 Additional Setup Considerations

◼ Set Up Default Views for Spaces and Folders

- Choose **List View, Board View, or Timeline View** based on how your team works best.
- Example: Marketing teams may prefer **Board View**, while engineering teams rely on **Gantt Charts**.

◼ Enable ClickApps for Added Functionality

- ClickApps provide **extra features** like **Time Tracking, Automations, and Custom Fields**.
- Activate only the ClickApps **your team actually needs** to prevent clutter.

◼ Use Templates for Repetitive Workflows

- Save time by **creating templates** for common project structures.
- Example: Create a **"Product Launch Plan"** template with predefined tasks and dependencies.

Final Thoughts: Building a Strong ClickUp Foundation

Setting up **Workspaces, Spaces, and Folders correctly** is crucial to ensuring **long-term success in ClickUp**. When done right, your team will experience:
◼ **Faster onboarding and adoption**
◼ **Clearer project visibility**
◼ **Seamless collaboration and workflow automation**

Now that you have a solid ClickUp structure, the next chapter will **focus on building a scalable hierarchy** that allows your team to handle increasing project complexity without losing control.

Structuring Your Hierarchy for Scalability

One of the biggest challenges in project management is **maintaining clarity and structure as projects grow**. Without a well-thought-out hierarchy, teams can quickly face:

✘ Disorganized tasks and overlapping work
✘ Difficulty in tracking dependencies
✘ Poor collaboration across departments
✘ A loss of visibility into project progress

ClickUp's **flexible hierarchy** is designed to accommodate projects of all sizes. Whether you're managing **a single team or a multi-department enterprise**, creating a **scalable** and **efficient** hierarchy is key to long-term success.

In this chapter, we'll explore:
■ The **best practices** for structuring ClickUp's hierarchy
■ How to **balance simplicity and scalability**
■ Common **hierarchical models for complex projects**

📌 Understanding ClickUp's Hierarchical Structure

ClickUp's hierarchy consists of multiple levels that allow for **both high-level planning and granular task tracking**. Here's how it works:

1 Workspaces (The Company-Wide Level)

- The **top-most level** of the hierarchy.
- Represents **your entire organization** or a large business unit.
- **Best Practice:** Keep **one Workspace per organization** to ensure smooth collaboration.

2 Spaces (The Department or Team Level)

- Spaces act as **separate divisions** for teams, functions, or large projects.
- Examples:
  ■ *Marketing*
  ■ *Product Development*
  ■ *Client Workflows*
  ■ *IT & Support*
- **Best Practice:** Use Spaces to separate **high-level categories of work** while keeping workflows independent.

3 Folders (The Project or Initiative Level)

- Folders **group related Lists** under a common theme.
- Examples:
  ■ *Software Development* (for Product Team)
  ■ *Ad Campaigns* (for Marketing Team)
  ■ *Client Onboarding* (for Customer Success Team)
- **Best Practice:** If a Space contains **multiple long-term projects**, use Folders for better organization.

4 Lists (The Execution Level)

- Lists are where **actual tasks live** and serve as an action hub.
- Each List represents **a specific project or phase**.

- Examples:
  - ■ *Sprint #1* (for Agile teams)
  - ■ *Website Redesign* (for a marketing project)
  - ■ *Customer Onboarding Tasks* (for support teams)
- **Best Practice:** Use **Lists to separate different workflows within a Folder** for easy tracking.

5 Tasks & Subtasks (The Detailed Work Level)

- Tasks are **actionable items** assigned to individuals or teams.
- Subtasks help **break down complex work** into smaller steps.
- **Best Practice:** Use **task dependencies** to ensure proper sequencing of work.

📌 Best Practices for Structuring a Scalable Hierarchy

A well-designed hierarchy should be:
■ **Clear** – Everyone understands where work belongs.
■ **Scalable** – It adapts as teams and projects grow.
■ **Efficient** – No duplication or unnecessary complexity.

Here are key tips to structure ClickUp effectively:

1 Define Your Organizational Needs First

Before setting up ClickUp, ask:

- **How is your company structured?** (By departments, projects, clients?)
- **Who needs visibility into which areas?**
- **How do different teams collaborate?**

Understanding these factors will guide your **Space and Folder setup**.

2 Keep Spaces High-Level, Not Overcomplicated

- **Good Example:**
■ *Tech Company:*

  - Space: **Engineering**
    - ○ Folder: *Product Development*
    - ○ Folder: *Bug Tracking*

- **Bad Example:**
✗ *Too Many Spaces for Small Tasks*

  - Space: **Feature A Development**
  - Space: **Feature B Bug Fixes**
  - Space: **Sprint #1**

👉 **Solution:** Use **Lists and Tags instead of creating excessive Spaces.**

3 Use Folders to Organize Long-Term Projects

If a Space has **multiple independent projects**, Folders provide an extra **layer of categorization**.

📌 Example for a Marketing Agency

- Space: **Client Campaigns**

- ○ Folder: *Social Media Projects*
  - ■ List: Facebook Ads
  - ■ List: Twitter Campaign
- ○ Folder: *SEO Projects*
  - ■ List: Blog Content Strategy
  - ■ List: Keyword Research

👉 **This structure keeps work organized without unnecessary complexity.**

4 Use Lists for Task Categorization, Not Over-Segmentation

Lists should serve as **groupings of related work**, not micro-divisions.

- ◆ **Good Example (for a Software Development Team):**

  - ● Folder: *Sprint Planning*
    - ○ List: *Sprint #1 Tasks*
    - ○ List: *Sprint #2 Tasks*

- ◆ **Bad Example:**
  ✗ A separate List for every small task category, leading to clutter.

👉 **Solution:** Use **Filters and Custom Fields** instead of excessive Lists.

5 Use Task Dependencies for Complex Workflows

Many complex projects involve **tasks that depend on others**. ClickUp allows you to:
■ Set **"Blocking" and "Waiting On" relationships**
■ Use **Gantt charts** to visualize dependencies
■ Automate **status changes** when dependencies are completed

📌 **Example:**

- ● Task 1: *Design Mockups* → Blocking Task 2
- ● Task 2: *Stakeholder Approval* → Blocking Task 3
- ● Task 3: *Website Development*

👉 **This ensures teams work in the correct order without bottlenecks.**

6 Use Custom Fields and Tags to Minimize Clutter

Instead of **creating unnecessary Spaces, Folders, or Lists**, use:
📌 **Custom Fields** – Track budget, priority, or assigned department.
📌 **Tags** – Label tasks with relevant identifiers (e.g., "Urgent", "Client A").

👉 **This keeps projects manageable without unnecessary segmentation.**

7 Use Templates to Standardize Project Structures

For recurring projects, **save structured Folders, Lists, and Task setups as templates**.

📌 **Example:**
■ *Product Launch Plan Template*
■ *New Client Onboarding Workflow*
■ *Content Production Pipeline*

👉 **This ensures consistency and speeds up project initiation.**

🚀 Putting It All Together: Example Hierarchies

Example 1: Corporate Team Structure (Department-Based)

📌 **Workspace: ABC Corp**

- Space: **Marketing**
  - Folder: *Campaign Management*
    - List: *Social Media Ads*
    - List: *Content Marketing*
  - Folder: *SEO & Growth*
- Space: **Engineering**
  - Folder: *Software Development*
  - Folder: *Bug Tracking*

Example 2: Client-Based Agency Structure

📌 **Workspace: XYZ Consulting**

- Space: **Client A – Digital Marketing**
  - Folder: *SEO & Ads*
    - List: *Google Ads*
    - List: *LinkedIn Campaigns*
- Space: **Client B – Product Launch**
  - Folder: *Branding & Design*
  - Folder: *Web Development*

Final Thoughts: Scaling ClickUp for Long-Term Growth

By implementing a **structured, scalable hierarchy**, your team will:
■ Reduce clutter and confusion
■ Improve cross-team collaboration
■ Scale projects without losing organization

In the next chapter, we'll dive into **how to customize ClickUp Views** to fit different project types, ensuring **optimal visibility for different teams.**

Customizing Views for Different Project Types

One of ClickUp's **greatest strengths** is its ability to **adapt to different workflows** through customizable views. Every team within an organization has **unique project management needs**, and a one-size-fits-all approach doesn't work for complex projects.

With ClickUp's **versatile views**, you can tailor how information is displayed for **different teams, workflows, and project types**—ensuring everyone can work in the most efficient way possible.

In this chapter, we will explore:
■ The **different ClickUp views** and when to use them
■ **Best practices** for tailoring views based on project type
■ How to **set default views** for your teams
■ Tips to **optimize productivity with custom views**

📌 Understanding ClickUp's View Options

ClickUp provides multiple views to **organize, visualize, and track projects** in a way that suits your workflow.

1 List View (Best for Detailed Task Management)

✔ **What It's For:**

- A structured, spreadsheet-like view for tracking tasks.
- Ideal for teams that need a **task-by-task breakdown** with columns for assignees, due dates, priorities, and more.

✔ **Best Used For:**
■ **Operations teams** tracking daily tasks
■ **HR and recruitment** pipelines
■ **Finance teams** managing budgets

✔ **Customization Tips:**

- Use **Custom Fields** to track unique data points like budget, urgency, or approval status.
- Apply **Filters** to view only high-priority tasks or upcoming deadlines.

---

2 Board View (Best for Agile & Kanban Workflows)

✔ **What It's For:**

- A **Kanban-style** layout that allows tasks to move across columns based on their status.
- Great for **visualizing workflows and tracking progress** in an intuitive way.

✔ **Best Used For:**
■ **Software development teams** following Agile or Scrum
■ **Marketing teams** tracking campaign progress
■ **Creative teams** managing content production

✔ **Customization Tips:**

- Set up columns based on **custom statuses** (e.g., "To Do," "In Progress," "Review," "Completed").

- Enable **Work in Progress (WIP) limits** to ensure teams don't take on too much at once.

---

③ Calendar View (Best for Scheduling & Deadline Management)

✔ **What It's For:**

- Provides a **time-focused** view of tasks based on due dates.
- Helps teams **track deadlines, plan sprints, and schedule events**.

✔ **Best Used For:**
■ **Event planning teams** managing schedules
■ **Content creators** tracking editorial calendars
■ **Project managers** planning delivery timelines

✔ **Customization Tips:**

- Sync with **Google Calendar** for real-time updates.
- Use **color-coded tags** to differentiate between task types.

---

④ Gantt Chart View (Best for Timeline & Dependency Tracking)

✔ **What It's For:**

- A **timeline-based visualization** that shows task dependencies and progress.
- Essential for teams managing **long-term projects with multiple phases**.

✔ **Best Used For:**
■ **Construction projects** managing multiple phases
■ **Software development teams** tracking product roadmaps
■ **Event organizers** ensuring all steps align for a big launch

✔ **Customization Tips:**

- **Enable Dependencies** to set "Blocking" and "Waiting On" relationships.
- Adjust **Critical Path Highlighting** to identify high-priority tasks.

---

⑤ Timeline View (Best for Managing Workloads Over Time)

✔ **What It's For:**

- Similar to Gantt View but focused on **team workloads and capacity planning**.
- Helps managers distribute tasks effectively across team members.

✔ **Best Used For:**
■ **Operations managers** balancing workload across teams
■ **HR departments** planning employee shifts
■ **Freelance agencies** assigning client projects

✔ **Customization Tips:**

- Drag and drop tasks to **adjust schedules on the fly**.
- Use **Resource View** to ensure no one is overbooked.

6 Dashboard View (Best for High-Level Insights & Reporting)

✔ **What It's For:**

- A **customizable analytics hub** for tracking project metrics, KPIs, and performance.
- Helps leadership teams monitor progress **without diving into task details**.

✔ **Best Used For:**
■ **Executive teams** needing a high-level overview
■ **Project managers** tracking task completion rates
■ **Scrum masters** measuring sprint velocity

✔ **Customization Tips:**

- Add **progress bars, pie charts, and workload distribution widgets**.
- Share dashboards with stakeholders for **real-time reporting**.

📌 How to Customize Views for Different Project Types

ClickUp's views can be customized to **fit the specific needs of your team**. Below are examples of **best view setups for different project types**.

1 Agile Development Team (Scrum/Kanban Approach)

📌 **Recommended Views:**
■ **Board View** – Organizes tasks by status (Backlog, In Progress, Done)
■ **List View** – Displays sprint tasks in a structured format
■ **Gantt View** – Tracks roadmap and feature releases

✔ **Customization Tips:**

- Set up **Automations** to move tasks automatically when a status changes.
- Use **Custom Fields** to track task effort (Story Points, Sprint #).

---

2 Marketing Campaign Management

📌 **Recommended Views:**
■ **Calendar View** – Tracks campaign launch dates
■ **List View** – Organizes tasks by channel (SEO, Social, Email)
■ **Dashboard View** – Provides real-time engagement and ROI tracking

✔ **Customization Tips:**

- Use **Tags** to categorize tasks by campaign type (Paid Ads, Organic, PR).
- Set up **Recurring Tasks** for ongoing efforts like weekly blog posts.

---

3 Client-Based Consulting or Freelance Work

📌 **Recommended Views:**
■ **Board View** – Tracks different client projects

■ **Timeline View** – Manages time allocation per client
■ **Dashboard View** – Provides an overview of billable vs. non-billable hours

✔ **Customization Tips:**

- Use **Custom Statuses** (Proposal, In Progress, Delivered).
- Integrate with **Slack or Email** for real-time client updates.

📌 Setting Default Views for Your Team

ClickUp allows you to **set default views** so that teams always see the most relevant layout when opening a Space, Folder, or List.

✔ **How to Set Default Views:**
1 Go to the **desired Space, Folder, or List**
2 Click on **"Views"** and select the most suitable one
3 Click **"Set as Default"** for all team members

- **Example:** If your team follows an Agile workflow, **set the Board View as the default** to instantly see task progress.

🚀 Final Thoughts: Maximizing Productivity with Custom Views

Customizing ClickUp views **empowers teams** to work efficiently by providing:
■ **Tailored experiences** that match their workflows
■ **Better project visibility** for different stakeholders
■ **Increased efficiency** by reducing time spent searching for information

In the next chapter, we'll **explore how to import existing data** into ClickUp, making your transition seamless and efficient.

Importing Existing Data into ClickUp

Transitioning to ClickUp from another project management tool—or even from spreadsheets and manual tracking—requires careful **data migration** to ensure a smooth start. A well-planned import process prevents:

✗ **Data loss or duplication**
✗ **Incomplete task records**
✗ **Disruptions in workflow**

By **properly importing tasks, projects, and key information**, you ensure that your team can **seamlessly continue their work** without losing valuable historical data.

In this chapter, you'll learn:
■ **The different import methods available in ClickUp**
■ **How to migrate from other project management tools**
■ **Best practices for organizing imported data**
■ **Troubleshooting common import issues**

📌 Understanding ClickUp's Import Options

ClickUp provides **built-in import tools** to help you transfer data from various sources. Here are the primary methods:

1. **Native Imports** → One-click migration from popular project management tools.
2. **CSV File Import** → Upload tasks and project data in bulk.
3. **Manual Data Entry** → Recommended for small-scale projects.
4. **ClickUp API & Third-Party Integrations** → Advanced custom imports.

Each method serves **different use cases**, so let's explore them in detail.

📌 Method 1: Using ClickUp's Built-In Import Tool

ClickUp allows **direct imports** from several project management platforms, including:

■ Asana
■ Trello
■ Monday.com
■ Jira
■ Todoist

How to Import from Other Tools

1. **Navigate to ClickUp's Import Tool**

   - Go to **Settings > Import/Export**
   - Click **Import from Another App**

2. **Select Your Existing Tool**

   - Click on the tool you're migrating from.
   - Sign in to authorize the connection.

3 **Choose the Data to Import**

- Select **Workspaces, Lists, Tasks, and Custom Fields** to bring over.
- Review the settings to ensure all necessary data is included.

4 **Confirm and Run the Import**

- Click **Start Import** and wait for ClickUp to process the data.
- Once completed, review your imported tasks to verify accuracy.

Best Practices:
✔ **Clean up your existing tool** before importing to **avoid unnecessary clutter**.
✔ Ensure **task statuses align** with ClickUp's workflow.
✔ Assign **task owners and due dates** to prevent data gaps.

📌 **Method 2: Importing Data via CSV Files**

For teams migrating from spreadsheets or unsupported tools, **CSV import is the best option**.

How to Import a CSV File into ClickUp

1 **Prepare Your CSV File**

- Ensure columns include:
  - **Task Name**
  - **Description**
  - **Due Date**
  - **Assignee**
  - **Status**
- Format the file in a **comma-separated format (.csv)**.

2 **Go to ClickUp's Import Section**

- Navigate to **Settings > Import/Export > CSV Import**.
- Click **Upload File** and select your CSV file.

3 **Map Fields to ClickUp**

- ClickUp will prompt you to **match CSV columns** with ClickUp fields.
- Assign **Custom Fields** where necessary.

4 **Run the Import & Verify Data**

- Start the import process.
- After completion, review imported tasks to ensure **accuracy and completeness**.

Best Practices:
✔ **Remove unnecessary data** before import to avoid clutter.
✔ **Use consistent column names** to make mapping easier.
✔ If importing large datasets, **split files into smaller batches** to prevent errors.

📌 **Method 3: Manual Data Entry for Smaller Projects**

If your project is small or **highly customized**, manual entry may be the best option.

1 Create a New List in ClickUp

- Go to your **desired Space > Create New List**.
- Name it appropriately (e.g., *2024 Q1 Tasks*).

2 Add Tasks Manually

- Click **"New Task"** and enter:
  - ■ Task Name
  - ■ Description
  - ■ Status & Priority
  - ■ Assignee & Due Date

3 Use Bulk Actions for Faster Setup

- Select multiple tasks and update **due dates, assignees, and statuses** in bulk.

Best Practices:
✔ Use **Templates** to avoid repetitive manual entry.
✔ Apply **Custom Fields** for additional details.
✔ If importing from paper notes, use **ClickUp Docs** to store key info.

📌 Method 4: Using the ClickUp API for Custom Imports

For **large enterprises** or **custom workflows**, ClickUp's **API** allows advanced data migration.

📌 Best Used For:
- ■ **Migrating complex datasets** from multiple platforms
- ■ **Syncing ClickUp with external databases**
- ■ **Automating data transfers from proprietary systems**

🔗 **ClickUp API Documentation**: api.clickup.com

Common integrations include:
- ■ **Zapier** – Automates importing from Google Sheets, Airtable, and more.
- ■ **Make (formerly Integromat)** – Connects external databases.

Best Practices:
✔ Work with **a developer** if importing **custom data**.
✔ Use **batch imports** to prevent API limits.
✔ Test with a **small dataset first** before migrating everything.

📌 Post-Import Checklist: Organizing Imported Data

Once your data is imported, follow these steps to **ensure a smooth transition**:

■ Review Task Assignments

- Ensure tasks are assigned to the correct **owners and teams**.

■ Check Due Dates & Priorities

- Adjust deadlines to **match real-world project timelines**.

■ **Align Statuses with ClickUp Workflows**

- If needed, **modify ClickUp's statuses** to reflect your previous system.

■ **Enable Automations for Efficiency**

- Set up **automations** to move tasks based on progress.

■ **Use Dashboards for Quick Overview**

- Create a **Dashboard View** to track **imported data and team workload**.

🚀 **Final Thoughts: A Seamless Transition to ClickUp**

Importing existing data **correctly** into ClickUp ensures a **smooth transition** and prevents disruptions in ongoing work. Whether you're migrating from **another tool, a spreadsheet, or a custom system**, ClickUp's flexible import options make the process **fast and efficient**.

By following the best practices outlined in this chapter, your team can **hit the ground running** in ClickUp—without losing important project history.

Section 3:
Core Features for Project Management

Task Management: Breaking Down Complex Deliverables

In complex projects, **task management** is more than just creating a to-do list—it's about structuring work efficiently, ensuring **clear ownership**, tracking **dependencies**, and facilitating **collaboration across teams**. Without a proper task management system, teams face:

✘ **Unclear responsibilities** leading to bottlenecks
✘ **Missed deadlines** due to poor tracking
✘ **Disorganized workflows** that slow down progress
✘ **Overloaded team members** resulting in burnout

ClickUp provides **powerful task management tools** that help teams **break down large deliverables into manageable tasks**, making projects easier to track and execute.

In this chapter, we'll cover:
■ The **best practices for structuring tasks** in ClickUp
■ How to **use Subtasks, Checklists, and Dependencies**
■ Organizing tasks using **priorities, statuses, and tags**
■ How to **automate task management for efficiency**

📌 Breaking Down Complex Deliverables into Manageable Tasks

A well-organized project begins with **breaking down high-level deliverables** into smaller, **actionable tasks**. ClickUp provides a **flexible task structure** that allows for easy tracking.

1 Start with the High-Level Goal (Deliverable)

Before creating tasks, **identify the final deliverable** and **its key components**.

📌 Example:
A marketing team is planning a **Product Launch Campaign**. Instead of having a single task labeled *"Launch the Product"*, they should break it down into **smaller milestones**:

■ Develop marketing strategy
■ Create promotional materials
■ Launch ad campaigns
■ Organize a product webinar
■ Track campaign performance

Each milestone should then be further divided into **individual tasks** assigned to specific team members.

📌 Using ClickUp's Task Structure for Better Organization

ClickUp offers **multiple layers of task management** that help teams structure complex deliverables.

2 Creating Main Tasks

- Each **key deliverable** should be a **separate task**.
- Assign **owners, due dates, and priorities** to ensure accountability.

📌 **Example – Task for Product Launch Campaign:**
◼ Task: *Develop Marketing Strategy*

- Assignee: *Marketing Lead*
- Due Date: *March 10*
- Priority: *High*

---

3 Using Subtasks for Detailed Execution

Each task can be **broken into subtasks** to handle specific steps.

📌 **Example – Subtasks for 'Develop Marketing Strategy'**
◼ Subtask 1: *Conduct market research*
◼ Subtask 2: *Define target audience*
◼ Subtask 3: *Outline messaging framework*
◼ Subtask 4: *Prepare campaign timeline*

Best Practices:
✔ Assign subtasks to **different team members** to distribute work.
✔ Enable **subtask dependencies** to ensure work progresses in the right sequence.

---

4 Checklists for Repetitive Steps

For **recurring** or **process-based** tasks, ClickUp offers **checklists** to track step-by-step execution.

📌 **Example – Checklist for Publishing a Blog Post:**
◼ Write content draft
◼ Get approval from the editor
◼ Design accompanying graphics
◼ Publish on the website
◼ Share on social media

Best Practices:
✔ Use **checklists** for standardized workflows like **QA testing, approvals, and compliance steps**.
✔ Convert commonly used checklists into **Templates** for repeated use.

📌 Organizing and Prioritizing Tasks Efficiently

Effective task management requires **clear prioritization and categorization**. ClickUp provides tools like **Priorities, Statuses, and Tags** to organize work efficiently.

5 Setting Task Priorities

ClickUp offers **four priority levels** to help teams focus on **what matters most**:
● **Urgent** – Critical and time-sensitive

● **High** – Important but not immediate
● **Normal** – Standard priority work
● **Low** – Can be scheduled for later

📌 **Example:**
🚀 *Urgent:* Fix a website bug before a major launch
📢 *High:* Finalize marketing materials
■ *Normal:* Draft a new blog post
💡 *Low:* Research ideas for future campaigns

Best Practices:
✔ Assign **clear priorities** to prevent confusion on what to focus on first.
✔ Combine priorities with **due dates** for better scheduling.

---

6 Custom Statuses for Tracking Progress

Unlike traditional to-do lists, ClickUp allows teams to create **custom statuses** to reflect their **unique workflow**.

📌 **Example – Statuses for a Video Production Team:**
■ **To Do** → Video concept created
■ **In Progress** → Scriptwriting & filming
■ **Editing** → Post-production work
■ **Client Review** → Waiting for approval
■ **Completed** → Final version published

Best Practices:
✔ Keep statuses **simple and meaningful** (avoid unnecessary stages).
✔ Use **status automation** to move tasks forward as work progresses.

---

7 Categorizing Tasks with Tags

Tags help **group and filter** tasks across projects.

📌 **Example – Tags for a Marketing Campaign:**
● *#SocialMedia* → Tasks related to social content
● *#PaidAds* → Google & Facebook ad management
● *#SEO* → Keyword research and optimization

Best Practices:
✔ Use **consistent tag naming** to avoid confusion.
✔ Apply tags to **filter tasks quickly** when needed.

📌 Using Dependencies to Manage Task Flow

For complex projects, tasks often **depend on each other**. ClickUp's **task dependencies** prevent teams from working on incomplete tasks.

📌 **Example – Task Dependencies in Software Development:**
🚀 *Feature Design* → Must be completed before 🚀 *UI Development* → Must be completed before 🚀 *Final Testing*

Best Practices:

✔ Use **"Blocking" and "Waiting On"** indicators to track dependencies.

✔ Visualize dependencies with **Gantt Charts** to prevent delays.

📌 Automating Task Management for Efficiency

ClickUp's **Automations** help teams **save time and reduce manual effort**.

📌 Example – Automations for Task Management:

■ Automatically assign tasks to a team member when they move to **"In Progress"**.

■ Change the **priority to Urgent** when a deadline is approaching.

■ Send a **Slack notification** when a task is completed.

Best Practices:

✔ Automate repetitive actions to **eliminate manual updates**.

✔ Set up **reminders and notifications** to keep tasks on track.

🚀 Final Thoughts: Task Management That Drives Results

By effectively structuring **tasks, subtasks, priorities, and dependencies**, teams can:

■ **Ensure clarity** in task ownership

■ **Break down complex deliverables** into **actionable steps**

■ **Prioritize tasks effectively** for better time management

■ **Automate workflows** to reduce effort and errors

In the next chapter, we'll explore how ClickUp's **Docs feature** helps teams **centralize documentation** and streamline collaboration.

Using Docs for Centralized Documentation

In complex projects, information is often scattered across emails, shared drives, chat messages, and personal notes, leading to:

✗ **Lost or outdated information**
✗ **Misalignment between teams**
✗ **Inefficient workflows and delays**
✗ **Inconsistent project documentation**

ClickUp **Docs** provides a **centralized, collaborative, and easily accessible** solution to organize project-related documentation **all in one place**. With ClickUp Docs, teams can:

■ Store **important project documents** in a single, searchable location
■ **Collaborate in real-time** without switching between tools
■ **Link tasks and workflows directly** to documentation
■ Use **permissions and sharing options** to control document access

In this chapter, we'll explore:
■ **How to create and structure Docs** in ClickUp
■ **Best practices for organizing project documentation**
■ **How to use Docs for team collaboration**
■ **Linking Docs to tasks, projects, and workflows**

📌 Understanding ClickUp Docs: Features & Benefits

ClickUp Docs is more than just a **text editor**—it's a powerful tool for:

✔ **Project documentation** – Store project plans, guidelines, and reports.
✔ **Knowledge management** – Create company wikis, SOPs, and training materials.
✔ **Team collaboration** – Write and edit documents in real time with your team.
✔ **Task integration** – Link Docs directly to **ClickUp tasks, projects, and dashboards**.

ClickUp Docs **eliminates the need for external tools** like Google Docs or Notion, keeping everything within a single platform.

📌 Creating and Structuring Docs in ClickUp

ClickUp allows users to create **unlimited Docs**, organized into **structured pages and nested sub-pages**.

1 Creating a New Doc

To create a Doc:
1 Navigate to the **Docs** tab in the left-hand sidebar.
2 Click **New Doc** and give it a clear name.
3 Start typing or use **ClickUp's pre-built templates**.

📌 Example: Creating a Project Charter Document
■ Title: *Website Redesign Project Charter*
■ Section 1: *Project Goals*
■ Section 2: *Stakeholders & Responsibilities*

■ Section 3: *Project Timeline*
■ Section 4: *Budget & Resources*

---

2 Organizing Docs for Clarity

ClickUp allows you to **structure Docs into folders** for better organization.

📌 **Best Practices for Structuring Docs:**
✔ **Use categories to separate documentation types** (e.g., "Project Guidelines," "Meeting Notes," "Onboarding Docs").
✔ **Use nested pages for better organization** (e.g., a Doc for "Marketing Strategy" could have sub-pages for "SEO Plan" and "Social Media").
✔ **Color-code and label Docs** for quick identification.

* **Example Doc Structure for a Software Development Team:**
📁 **Product Documentation**

  * ■ *Feature Specs*
  * ■ *User Requirements*
  📁 **Meeting Notes**
  * ■ *Sprint Planning – March 2024*
  * ■ *Retrospective Notes*
  📁 **Standard Operating Procedures (SOPs)**
  * ■ *Code Deployment Guide*
  * ■ *Bug Reporting Process*

📌 **Best Practices for Using ClickUp Docs**

3 Make Docs Actionable with Embedded Tasks

ClickUp allows you to **embed tasks directly into Docs**, turning documentation into an interactive workflow.

📌 **Example – Actionable Meeting Notes:**
■ Meeting Agenda
■ Discussion Points
■ Action Items (linked to ClickUp Tasks)

How to Embed a Task in a Doc:
1 Type /task inside a Doc.
2 Select an **existing task** or **create a new one**.
3 Assign it to a team member with a due date.

■ This ensures that **decisions turn into action items** without switching between tools.

---

4 Use Real-Time Collaboration for Teamwork

ClickUp Docs supports:
✔ **Live editing** – Team members can edit Docs simultaneously.
✔ **Comments & Mentions** – Add comments and tag teammates for discussions.
✔ **Version history** – Track changes and revert to previous versions if needed.

📌 **Example – Collaborative Marketing Strategy Doc:**
■ @mention a designer to provide feedback on ad creatives.
■ Leave comments for stakeholders to approve campaign details.
■ Track changes to review previous iterations of the document.

---

5 **Control Access with Permissions**

Not all Docs should be accessible to everyone. ClickUp allows **granular permissions**, ensuring the right people have the right access.

📌 **Permission Levels in ClickUp Docs:**
■ **Full Access** – Can edit and manage Docs.
■ **Edit Only** – Can edit content but not delete or share.
■ **Comment Only** – Can leave feedback but not modify content.
■ **View Only** – Read access only.

 • **Example:** A company wiki can be **View Only** for general employees but **Editable** for managers.

📌 **Linking Docs to Tasks, Projects, and Workflows**

One of ClickUp Docs' most powerful features is the ability to **connect documentation directly to tasks and projects**.

6 **Attach Docs to Tasks for Easy Reference**

📌 **Example – Attaching a Requirements Doc to a Task:**
■ **Task:** "Develop New Homepage Design"
■ **Attached Doc:** *Homepage Wireframe Guidelines*

📌 **Steps to Attach a Doc to a Task:**
1 Open a ClickUp task.
2 Click **Attach > Docs**.
3 Select an existing Doc or create a new one.

■ This ensures that **team members always have the relevant documentation at hand.**

---

7 **Embed Docs in Dashboards for Quick Access**

ClickUp allows Docs to be embedded in **Dashboards**, giving teams quick access to key documentation.

📌 **Example – Using Docs in a Dashboard:**
■ A **Sales Dashboard** can include a "Sales Playbook Doc."
■ A **Development Dashboard** can link to "Sprint Documentation."

📌 **Using ClickUp Docs for Different Teams & Use Cases**

ClickUp Docs can be adapted for various teams and industries:

8 **Project Management Teams**

✔ Store **project charters, goals, and milestones**.
✔ Document **project meeting notes** and link to tasks.

9 Product & Development Teams

✔ Maintain **technical documentation** for features.
✔ Link **API docs to development tasks**.

■ Marketing Teams

✔ Keep a **content calendar Doc** linked to campaign tasks.
✔ Store **brand guidelines** for easy reference.

11 HR & Operations

✔ Create **employee onboarding Docs** for new hires.
✔ Store **company policies and handbooks**.

🚀 Final Thoughts: A Single Source of Truth

ClickUp Docs allows teams to:
■ **Centralize documentation** in a single, searchable place.
■ **Collaborate in real time** without switching between tools.
■ **Link Docs to tasks, projects, and dashboards** for seamless workflows.
■ **Use permissions** to control access and maintain security.

By leveraging ClickUp Docs effectively, teams **reduce information silos, increase collaboration**, and ensure **everyone stays aligned on project details**.

Timelines and Gantt Charts for Long-Term Planning

Long-term project planning is essential for **ensuring milestones are met, dependencies are accounted for, and workloads are balanced**. Without proper planning tools, teams may struggle with:

✗ **Missed deadlines due to poor task sequencing**
✗ **Unclear dependencies causing bottlenecks**
✗ **Overloaded team members and inefficient resource allocation**
✗ **Lack of visibility into project progress**

ClickUp provides **powerful timeline and Gantt chart features** to help teams **visualize project progress, manage dependencies, and track deadlines effectively**.

In this chapter, you'll learn:
■ **The difference between Timelines and Gantt Charts**
■ **How to create and customize Gantt Charts in ClickUp**
■ **Best practices for using Timelines for strategic planning**
■ **How to track dependencies and adjust schedules dynamically**

📌 Understanding ClickUp's Timeline vs. Gantt View

ClickUp offers **two primary views for long-term planning**:

Feature	Timeline View	Gantt View
Purpose	Scheduling tasks over time	Visualizing dependencies & project roadmap
Best For	Assigning tasks over days/weeks	Managing complex, multi-phase projects
Dependency Tracking	No	Yes
Critical Path Highlighting	No	Yes
Adjustable Task Durations	Yes	Yes
Drag-and-Drop Scheduling	Yes	Yes

Both views allow for **interactive planning**, but Gantt Charts are better for **projects with dependencies and milestones**, while Timelines are better for **resource and workload management**.

📌 Creating a Gantt Chart in ClickUp

1 Enabling Gantt View

To activate the Gantt View:
1 Navigate to your **Project Space or Folder**.
2 Click on **"+ View"** at the top.
3 Select **"Gantt"** and click **Add View**.

Now, you have a **Gantt chart layout displaying tasks as horizontal bars across a timeline**.

2 Adding Tasks and Dependencies

1 **Ensure all tasks have start and due dates** – Gantt charts won't display tasks without assigned dates.
2 Click and drag **task bars** to adjust dates dynamically.
3 **Add dependencies** by dragging a line from one task to another.

📌 **Example – Managing a Product Launch with a Gantt Chart:**
🚀 *Task 1: Develop marketing strategy* → Must be completed before 🚀 *Task 2: Start ad campaigns* → Must be completed before 🚀 *Task 3: Launch event*

Best Practices:
✔ Use **dependencies** to indicate blocking tasks.
✔ Set **realistic deadlines** to avoid unrealistic project expectations.

3 Adjusting Schedules Dynamically

ClickUp's Gantt Chart allows for **easy timeline adjustments**:

📌 **How to Reschedule Tasks Efficiently:**
■ Drag and drop task bars to extend or reduce task duration.
■ Shift entire groups of tasks forward or backward as needed.
■ Use the **Critical Path Feature** to identify **tasks that directly impact project completion**.

♦ **Example:** If a **design phase** is delayed, ClickUp automatically **adjusts all dependent tasks accordingly**.

📌 Using Timeline View for Long-Term Scheduling

4 Enabling Timeline View

To enable Timeline View:
1 Click **"+ View"** on a Folder or Space.
2 Select **"Timeline"** and click **Add View**.

📌 **Best Use Cases for Timeline View:**
■ Managing **employee workload** over multiple projects
■ Planning **editorial calendars** for content teams
■ Scheduling **event logistics** over weeks or months

Unlike Gantt View, Timeline View does **not show dependencies**, making it ideal for **high-level scheduling**.

5 Distributing Workloads Over Time

ClickUp's **drag-and-drop interface** lets you **reassign or reschedule tasks** based on team availability.

📌 **Example – Workload Balancing for a Development Team:**
♦ *Developer A:* Assigned **Task A, B, and C**
♦ *Developer B:* Assigned **Task D and E**

If Developer A is overloaded, simply **drag Task C to Developer B's timeline** for a balanced workload.

Best Practices:
✔ Keep an eye on **team availability** when assigning long-term projects.
✔ Use **Custom Fields** for tracking project phases (e.g., "Planning," "Execution," "Review").

📌 Tracking Milestones & Critical Path for Project Success

6 Setting Project Milestones

Milestones represent **key deadlines or checkpoints** in a project.

📌 Example – Milestones for a Software Development Project:
■ *Milestone 1:* Finish initial UI design
■ *Milestone 2:* Complete first round of beta testing
■ *Milestone 3:* Final product launch

◆ **How to Add a Milestone in ClickUp:**
1 Open a **Gantt Chart**.
2 Click **New Task > Convert to Milestone**.
3 Assign it a deadline and track progress.

Best Practices:
✔ Use **Milestones to communicate key deadlines** with stakeholders.
✔ Highlight **critical milestones** in reports for better visibility.

---

7 Using the Critical Path Method for Priority Tracking

ClickUp's **Critical Path Feature** helps teams identify **the most important tasks affecting deadlines**.

📌 How to Enable Critical Path in Gantt View:
1 Open your **Gantt Chart**.
2 Click **"More" > Enable Critical Path**.
3 ClickUp will highlight **tasks that directly impact project completion**.

◆ **Example:** If a coding task is delayed, **it might push the entire software launch back**, making it a **critical path task**.

✔ **Best Practice:** Always **prioritize** tasks on the critical path to avoid project delays.

📌 Automating Long-Term Planning with ClickUp's Features

To enhance long-term planning efficiency, ClickUp offers:

■ **Recurring Tasks** – Automate repeated activities (e.g., weekly progress reviews).
■ **Task Templates** – Save project workflows for future use.
■ **Automations** – Trigger notifications for approaching deadlines.

📌 Example – Automating a Content Calendar:
✔ *Set a recurring task* for monthly content planning.
✔ *Automate due date reminders* for writers and designers.

🚀 Final Thoughts: Mastering Long-Term Planning in ClickUp

By leveraging **Timelines and Gantt Charts**, teams can:
- **Gain visibility into project timelines** and adjust schedules dynamically.
- **Manage dependencies effectively** to prevent bottlenecks.
- **Balance workloads** across team members efficiently.
- **Track milestones and critical paths** to ensure projects stay on track.

In the next chapter, we'll explore **how to automate repetitive processes** in ClickUp to save time and increase efficiency.

Automations to Reduce Manual Work

Managing complex projects often involves **repetitive administrative tasks** such as updating statuses, assigning tasks, sending reminders, and tracking progress. These manual processes can **slow down teams, introduce human errors, and waste valuable time**.

ClickUp's **Automation** feature helps teams **streamline workflows, eliminate repetitive work, and increase overall efficiency**.

With automations, you can:
- Automatically **assign tasks** based on status updates
- Change **priorities** dynamically when due dates are near
- Trigger **notifications** when tasks move to different stages
- Set up **recurring tasks** without manual input

In this chapter, you'll learn:
- **How ClickUp's Automations Work**
- **Common Automation Use Cases**
- **Best Practices for Setting Up Automations**
- **How to Use Automations for Scaling Workflows**

📌 Understanding ClickUp's Automation System

ClickUp automations work on a **Trigger → Condition → Action** system.

- **Trigger** – The event that starts the automation (e.g., Task Status changes).
- **Condition** – Optional rules that refine when the action should occur (e.g., Only applies to tasks marked "Urgent").
- **Action** – The task ClickUp will complete automatically (e.g., Assign task to a specific team member).

- **Example:**

Trigger: When a task moves to "In Progress" → **Action**: Assign the task to the team lead.

📌 Common Automation Use Cases

1 Auto-Assigning Tasks Based on Status Changes

📌 **Example:**
Trigger: When a task moves to "In Review"
Action: Assign the task to a reviewer.

💡 **Best Practice:**
✔ Ensure all team members **understand their responsibilities** in status-based assignments.

---

2 Changing Priorities Dynamically

📌 **Example:**
Trigger: When a task is **1 day before the due date**
Action: Change priority to "Urgent"

♥ Best Practice:
✔ Set priority adjustments **at least 2-3 days before a deadline** to allow teams to react.

---

③ Sending Notifications for Important Updates

📌 Example:
■ **Trigger**: When a task is moved to "Blocked"
■ **Action**: Send a Slack message to the project manager.

♥ Best Practice:
✔ Avoid **overloading teams** with too many notifications—send only critical alerts.

---

④ Automating Task Recurrence

📌 Example:
■ **Trigger**: When a task is marked "Complete"
■ **Action**: Create a duplicate task for the **next week/month**.

♥ Best Practice:
✔ Use recurring tasks for **regular reporting, content creation, or maintenance work**.

---

⑤ Moving Tasks Based on Dependencies

📌 Example:
■ **Trigger**: When "Task A" is completed
■ **Action**: Move "Task B" to "To Do."

♥ Best Practice:
✔ Use **Gantt Charts to visualize** how tasks interact with one another.

📌 Setting Up Automations in ClickUp

Step 1: Open the Automation Menu

① Navigate to a **List, Folder, or Space** where you want automations.
② Click the **"Automate"** button in the top bar.
③ Click **"Add Automation"** to begin.

Step 2: Choose a Pre-Made or Custom Automation

- ClickUp offers **pre-built automation templates** for common workflows.
- For advanced users, create a **custom automation** using **Triggers, Conditions, and Actions**.

Step 3: Customize the Automation

① Select the **Trigger (e.g., Status changes, Due Date approaching, etc.)**
② Add **Conditions** (optional) to filter when the automation applies.
③ Choose an **Action** (e.g., Assign task, change priority, send notification).

Step 4: Test & Activate

✔ Before rolling out automations, test them with **a small sample of tasks**.
✔ Monitor automation logs in ClickUp to **ensure they work as expected**.

📌 Best Practices for Using Automations

- **Keep Automations Simple**

■ Don't overcomplicate workflows—start with **basic automations** before adding advanced logic.

- **Combine Automations with Custom Fields**

■ Use custom fields like **Task Owner, Priority, or Due Date** to fine-tune automation rules.

- **Monitor & Adjust Over Time**

■ Review your automation settings **every quarter** to ensure they still align with team workflows.

- **Use Automations to Reduce, Not Replace, Human Oversight**

■ Automations should **support decision-making, not eliminate it**. Ensure critical approvals still require human input.

📌 Advanced Automation Strategies for Scaling Workflows

For teams managing **complex projects**, ClickUp offers **multi-step automations** to streamline work even further.

1️⃣ Multi-Step Automation Example: Automating a Content Approval Workflow

📌 **Scenario:** A marketing team wants to automate blog content approvals.

■ **Trigger**: When a content draft moves to "Ready for Review."
■ **Action 1**: Assign task to **Editor**.
■ **Action 2**: Change due date to **3 days from now**.
■ **Action 3**: Send Slack message to notify team.

💡 **Best Practice:**
✔ Use multi-step automations for **multi-person approvals or sequential task hand-offs**.

2️⃣ Combining Automations with Integrations

ClickUp can **connect automations to external tools** like Slack, Email, and Google Drive.

📌 **Example – Automating Meeting Follow-Ups:**
■ **Trigger**: When a meeting task is marked "Complete."
■ **Action 1**: Send a follow-up email to attendees.
■ **Action 2**: Attach meeting notes from Google Docs.

💡 **Best Practice:**
✔ Integrate ClickUp with **Zapier** or native integrations for more powerful automations.

🚀 Final Thoughts: Automating Workflows for Maximum Efficiency

By leveraging **ClickUp's automation features**, teams can:

- **Reduce manual work** and minimize human errors.
- **Speed up repetitive processes**, freeing up time for strategic tasks.
- **Improve project consistency**, ensuring workflows run smoothly.
- **Scale efficiently** by setting up **multi-step automations** for complex operations.

In the next chapter, we'll explore **how to use Custom Fields to create tailored workflows that fit your team's unique needs**.

Custom Fields for Tailored Workflows

Every project is unique, and standard task fields like **title, assignee, due date, and priority** may not be enough to track the specific details your team needs. ClickUp's **Custom Fields** allow teams to **create tailored workflows**, ensuring that critical information is captured and tasks are managed effectively.

With **Custom Fields**, you can:
- Track **budget, estimated hours, or project phase**
- Assign **custom statuses or categorization labels**
- Filter and sort tasks **based on project-specific criteria**
- Streamline reporting and dashboards with **customized data points**

In this chapter, you'll learn:
- **What Custom Fields are and how they work**
- **The different types of Custom Fields**
- **How to create and apply Custom Fields**
- **Best practices for structuring Custom Fields**
- **Real-world examples of Custom Fields in action**

📌 Understanding Custom Fields in ClickUp

Custom Fields provide **extra layers of data** for tasks, lists, and projects, making ClickUp a truly **flexible project management solution**.

Without Custom Fields:
- ✗ Teams must rely on **task descriptions** for additional details.
- ✗ Information is **scattered** across multiple locations.
- ✗ Sorting and filtering tasks based on unique criteria is **challenging**.

With Custom Fields:
- Teams can **customize their task structure** to fit their workflow.
- Key information is **visible at a glance**.
- Tasks can be **sorted, filtered, and reported on efficiently**.

- ◆ **Example:** A construction company might need to track **material costs, vendor names, and delivery dates**, while a marketing team might need to log **ad campaign budget, engagement rates, and social media platforms**.

📌 Types of Custom Fields in ClickUp

ClickUp offers several **types of Custom Fields** to match different data-tracking needs:

Custom Field Type	Use Case Example
Text	Add extra notes like "Client Name" or "Project Phase".
Dropdown	Categorize tasks (e.g., "High", "Medium", "Low" priority).
Number	Track numerical values such as budgets or hours worked.

Date	Add custom deadlines, meeting dates, or launch dates.
Checkbox	Indicate whether a step has been completed (e.g., "Reviewed by Manager").
Labels	Tag tasks with multiple attributes (e.g., "Marketing," "Sales," "Design").
Formula	Perform calculations (e.g., Cost = Hours Worked × Hourly Rate).
Progress Bar	Track task or project completion percentages.
People	Assign multiple people outside standard assignees (e.g., "Stakeholders").
Monetary	Track revenue, expenses, or costs for finance-related tasks.

💡 **Best Practice: Choose the right Custom Field type based on how you want to sort, filter, and report your data.**

📌 How to Create and Apply Custom Fields in ClickUp

1 Adding Custom Fields to a List or Folder

1 Navigate to your **desired List or Folder**.
2 Click on **"+ Add Column"** in List View.
3 Select **"Custom Field"** and choose a field type.
4 Name the field (e.g., "Client Name" or "Estimated Budget").
5 Click **Save** to apply it to all tasks in the List or Folder.

💡 **Tip:** Custom Fields added at the **Folder level** apply to all Lists inside it.

---

2 Applying Custom Fields Across Multiple Projects

To **reuse** Custom Fields across projects:
1 Go to **Settings > Custom Fields**.
2 Save a Custom Field as a **Template** for future use.
3 Apply the Template to any List or Space where you need the field.

📌 **Example – Applying a "Budget" Field Across Teams:**
■ **Marketing Team:** Tracks **Ad Spend** and **ROI**.
■ **Product Development Team:** Tracks **R&D Budget**.
■ **Finance Team:** Tracks **Overall Company Expenses**.

---

3 Filtering and Sorting Tasks with Custom Fields

Once Custom Fields are added, teams can:
✔ **Filter tasks** to show only relevant entries (e.g., "Only show tasks with budgets over $10,000").

✔ **Sort lists** based on a specific field (e.g., "Show tasks sorted by highest estimated hours first").
✔ **Group tasks** by Custom Fields (e.g., "Group by Project Phase").

📌 **Example – Managing an Agile Sprint:**
◼ Create a **Dropdown Field** for task type (Bug, Feature, Enhancement).
◼ Filter the sprint board to **only show Features** in progress.
◼ Use a **Progress Bar Field** to track sprint completion.

📌 **Best Practices for Using Custom Fields**

♦ ⓵ **Keep Custom Fields Organized**
◼ Use **consistent naming conventions** (e.g., "Project Start Date" instead of "Start").
◼ Limit the number of fields per list—**too many fields create clutter**.

♦ ⓶ **Use Dropdowns Instead of Free-Text Fields**
◼ Dropdown fields ensure **data consistency** across teams.
✘ Free-text fields allow **variations and errors** (e.g., "High Priority" vs. "HIGH").

♦ ⓷ **Utilize Formulas for Automated Calculations**
◼ Use **Formula Fields** to auto-calculate budgets or costs (e.g., "Hourly Rate × Hours Worked").

♦ ⓸ **Apply Custom Fields to Dashboards for Real-Time Tracking**
◼ Create a **Dashboard Widget** to track all high-priority tasks.
◼ Display **financial projections** based on the Monetary Field.

📌 **Real-World Use Cases for Custom Fields**

♦ ◼ **Project Management Teams**
✔ Track **project budgets, phases, and key deadlines**.
✔ Categorize tasks by **department or priority**.

♦ 📢 **Marketing & Content Teams**
✔ Track **content types (Blog, Video, Ad Campaign)**.
✔ Assign **review status (Draft, Editing, Published)**.

♦ 🏭 **IT & Development Teams**
✔ Identify **bug severity levels (Critical, Major, Minor)**.
✔ Track **code review status** with a checkbox.

♦ ⬢ **E-Commerce & Operations**
✔ Track **inventory stock levels** with a Number Field.
✔ Use a **Date Field** for **shipment tracking**.

♦ 💰 **Finance Teams**
✔ Monitor **projected vs. actual budgets** using **Formula Fields**.
✔ Add **Monetary Fields** to track revenue per project.

🚀 **Final Thoughts: Maximizing Efficiency with Custom Fields**

By implementing **Custom Fields strategically**, teams can:
◼ **Capture project-specific data** efficiently.

- ■ **Sort, filter, and automate** tasks based on custom criteria.
- ■ **Improve reporting** with tailored fields for dashboards.
- ■ **Scale workflows across multiple projects** seamlessly.

In the next chapter, we'll explore **how to use Priorities and Statuses to track project progress more effectively.**

Priorities and Statuses to Track Progress

In complex projects, **tracking progress accurately is critical** to ensure deadlines are met and bottlenecks are minimized. Without a clear priority and status system, teams often face:

✗ **Unclear task urgency** leading to missed deadlines
✗ **Confusion over task progress** causing duplicated work
✗ **Lack of visibility into overall project health**

ClickUp provides **two essential features—Priorities and Statuses—to help teams efficiently manage workflow tracking and ensure smooth task progression**.

In this chapter, we'll cover:
■ **How to use ClickUp Priorities effectively**
■ **Creating and customizing Statuses for different workflows**
■ **Filtering and reporting tasks based on Priorities and Statuses**
■ **Best practices for prioritization and status tracking**

📌 Understanding ClickUp Priorities

ClickUp's **Priority feature** helps teams identify and **focus on the most critical tasks first**. It provides a **four-tier priority system**:

Priority Level	Meaning	Example Use Case
● Urgent	Must be done ASAP	Fix a critical website bug
● High	Very important but not immediate	Approve an ad campaign before launch
● Normal	Standard tasks that need completion	Write a blog post
● Low	Not time-sensitive	Research future project ideas

📌 How to Set Priorities in ClickUp:
1️⃣ Open a task in ClickUp.
2️⃣ Click the **Priority Flag** icon.
3️⃣ Select the appropriate priority level.

💡 Best Practices:
✔ Assign **Urgent and High priorities sparingly** to maintain focus.
✔ Combine **Priorities with Due Dates** to ensure deadlines are met.
✔ Regularly **review priority levels** to adjust based on workload.

📌 Using Priorities to Improve Task Execution

1️⃣ Filtering Tasks by Priority

ClickUp allows you to filter tasks based on priority levels.

📌 **Example – Handling High-Priority Tasks First**
■ **Filter Tasks**: Show only tasks marked **Urgent** and **High**.
■ **Sort Tasks**: Arrange tasks by **Priority Level** to address critical work first.

💡 **Best Practices:**
✔ Use **Saved Filters** to quickly access high-priority tasks.
✔ Combine filters with **Due Dates** to spot overdue urgent tasks.

2️⃣ **Automating Priority-Based Actions**

ClickUp **Automations** can change priorities dynamically.

📌 **Example – Auto-Escalating Tasks Near Due Date**
■ **Trigger**: When a task is **2 days before due date**
■ **Action**: Change Priority to **Urgent**

💡 **Best Practices:**
✔ Set **reminders for upcoming deadlines** based on priority.
✔ Use **Dashboard Widgets** to highlight **high-priority open tasks**.

📌 **Understanding ClickUp Statuses**

Statuses indicate **where a task stands in its lifecycle**. They help teams **track progress and ensure nothing falls through the cracks**.

ClickUp provides **Custom Statuses** to match different workflows.

📌 **Example – Default Statuses in ClickUp**:
■ **To Do** → Task is not yet started.
■ **In Progress** → Work is actively being done.
■ **Review** → Task is under review or pending approval.
■ **Completed** → Task is finished.

📌 **Customizing Statuses for Different Teams**

ClickUp allows users to **customize task statuses** for different project types.

📌 **Example – Statuses for a Marketing Campaign**
◆ **Ideas** → Task is under brainstorming.
◆ **In Draft** → Initial content creation started.
◆ **Approval** → Awaiting client review.
◆ **Scheduled** → Ready for publishing.
◆ **Completed** → Campaign launched.

📌 **Example – Statuses for a Software Development Team**
◆ **Backlog** → Task is in the planning stage.
◆ **In Progress** → Currently being developed.
◆ **QA Testing** → Undergoing quality checks.
◆ **Deployment** → Being released to production.
◆ **Done** → Fully completed and live.

💡 Best Practices:
✔ Keep statuses **simple and logical** to avoid confusion.
✔ Use **status colors** to differentiate between workflow stages.
✔ Set up **automatic status transitions** based on task completion.

📌 Automating Status Changes for Efficiency

ClickUp allows teams to **automate status transitions** to minimize manual updates.

📌 Example – Automating a Content Approval Workflow
■ **Trigger**: When a task is moved to "In Review"
■ **Action**: Assign the task to a **Reviewer**

📌 Example – Auto-Moving Completed Tasks
■ **Trigger**: When a task is marked "Complete"
■ **Action**: Move it to the "Archived" list

💡 Best Practices:
✔ Automate repetitive workflows to **save time**.
✔ Ensure **stakeholders receive notifications** when status changes.

📌 Tracking Progress Using Priorities and Statuses

ClickUp provides **multiple ways to track project status using Priorities and Statuses**:

1 Using Dashboards to Monitor Project Health

ClickUp's **Dashboard View** provides **real-time insights** on task progress.

📌 Example – Setting Up a Priority-Based Dashboard
■ Create a **Task Progress Widget** filtered by **Urgent & High Priority**.
■ Add a **Pie Chart Widget** showing task distribution across statuses.

💡 Best Practices:
✔ Review dashboards weekly to identify **stalled tasks**.
✔ Share dashboards with **team leads** for better decision-making.

---

2 Reporting on Priorities and Statuses

ClickUp's **Custom Reports** allow teams to **generate insights based on task priorities and statuses**.

📌 Example – Generating a Priority Report for an Agile Sprint
■ Create a report showing **Urgent tasks by assignee**.
■ Identify overdue **High Priority** tasks.

💡 Best Practices:
✔ Use reports to spot **workload imbalances**.
✔ Adjust **team priorities based on data-driven insights**.

🚀 Final Thoughts: Optimizing Workflows with Priorities and Statuses

By using ClickUp's **Priorities and Statuses**, teams can:
- **Ensure task urgency is clearly defined.**
- **Track progress effectively using customized statuses.**
- **Automate workflows for faster execution.**
- **Leverage dashboards and reports for real-time insights.**

In the next chapter, we'll explore **how to manage dependencies and subtasks to ensure project success**.

Section 4:
Advanced Techniques for Complexity

Managing Dependencies and Subtasks

Complex projects require **structured task execution** where some tasks **depend on others to be completed first**. If teams don't manage dependencies properly, they can face:

✗ **Bottlenecks due to blocked tasks**
✗ **Confusion about task sequencing**
✗ **Missed deadlines due to poor planning**
✗ **Poor visibility into project progress**

ClickUp provides **powerful tools to manage dependencies and subtasks**, ensuring that work moves smoothly from one stage to the next.

In this chapter, we'll cover:
▇ **The difference between Dependencies and Subtasks**
▇ **How to set up Dependencies in ClickUp**
▇ **Using Subtasks to break down complex work**
▇ **Visualizing Dependencies with Gantt Charts**
▇ **Automating Dependencies for smoother workflows**

📌 Understanding Dependencies and Subtasks

Before diving into ClickUp's features, it's important to **differentiate** between Dependencies and Subtasks.

Feature	Purpose	Example
Dependencies	Ensures that one task cannot begin until another is completed.	"Design Approval" must be completed before "Website Development" starts.
Subtasks	Breaks down a large task into smaller, manageable steps.	A "Launch Marketing Campaign" task might include subtasks like "Write Copy," "Design Ads," and "Schedule Posts."

💡 **Best Practice: Use Dependencies for sequencing tasks across multiple people or teams, and Subtasks for breaking down complex tasks assigned to one team or individual.**

📌 Using Dependencies to Ensure Proper Task Flow

ClickUp provides **three types of Dependencies** to help teams manage project sequencing.

Dependency Type	Purpose	Example Use Case

Waiting On	Task cannot start until another task is completed.	"Develop Homepage" is waiting on "Approve Wireframe."
Blocking	Task must be completed before another can begin.	"Client Feedback" is blocking "Final Edits."
Linked To	Tasks are related but not dependent.	"Social Media Promo" is linked to "Email Announcement."

1 How to Set Dependencies in ClickUp

1 Open a **Task** in ClickUp.
2 Scroll to the **Dependencies** section.
3 Click **"+ Add Dependency"** and choose:

- **Waiting On** (If this task depends on another)
- **Blocking** (If this task must be done first)
- **Linked To** (If the task is related)

📌 **Example – Setting Up Dependencies for a Software Development Workflow:**
■ **Task 1:** Write Code *(Waiting On: UI Design Completion)*
■ **Task 2:** QA Testing *(Waiting On: Code Completion)*
■ **Task 3:** Deploy Software *(Waiting On: QA Testing Completion)*

💡 **Best Practice:** Always **review Dependencies before project kickoff** to avoid **unnecessary bottlenecks**.

📌 Using Subtasks to Break Down Complex Work

Subtasks help teams **divide large deliverables into smaller, actionable steps**.

📌 **Example – Breaking Down a "Launch Event" Task:**
■ **Main Task:** "Organize Product Launch Event"
- **Subtask 1:** Secure Venue
- **Subtask 2:** Send Invitations
- **Subtask 3:** Prepare Presentation
- **Subtask 4:** Coordinate Catering

2 How to Create Subtasks in ClickUp

1 Open a **Task**.
2 Click **"Add Subtask"**.
3 Name the subtask and assign an **Owner and Due Date**.
4 (Optional) Add **Dependencies** between Subtasks.

📌 **Example – Using Subtasks for an Ad Campaign:**
■ **Task:** "Execute Facebook Ad Campaign"
- Subtask: "Design Ad Creatives" *(Assigned to Graphic Designer)*
- Subtask: "Write Ad Copy" *(Assigned to Content Writer)*
- Subtask: "Launch Campaign" *(Assigned to Marketing Team)*

💡 **Best Practice:** Assign **each subtask** to a responsible team member and **set deadlines** to keep projects on schedule.

📌 Visualizing Dependencies with Gantt Charts

For complex projects, visualizing Dependencies in **Gantt View** helps teams track progress easily.

③ How to Use Gantt Charts for Dependencies

1️⃣ Go to the **Gantt View** in ClickUp.
2️⃣ Click on a task and drag a **Dependency Line** to another task.
3️⃣ ClickUp automatically adjusts **timelines when dependencies shift**.

📌 **Example – Managing a Marketing Campaign Timeline:**
■ Week 1: **Develop Creative Assets** *(Blocks Campaign Setup)*
■ Week 2: **Set Up Ad Targeting** *(Waiting On Assets Completion)*
■ Week 3: **Launch & Monitor Performance** *(Waiting On Setup Completion)*

💡 **Best Practice:** Use **Critical Path Highlighting** in Gantt View to identify tasks that could **delay the entire project**.

📌 Automating Dependencies for Efficiency

ClickUp allows teams to **automate dependencies** to reduce manual tracking.

④ Automating Task Movement Based on Dependency Completion

📌 **Example – Auto-Moving Tasks Forward**
■ **Trigger:** When Task A is marked "Complete"
■ **Action:** Move Task B to "In Progress"

📌 **Example – Automatic Task Assignments**
■ **Trigger:** When "Content Approval" is completed
■ **Action:** Assign "Publish Blog Post" to the content manager

💡 **Best Practice:** Automate routine task movements, but **keep key approvals manual** for better oversight.

📌 Best Practices for Managing Dependencies and Subtasks

◆ ① **Use Dependencies to Manage Sequential Workflows**
■ Always define dependencies **before project kickoff** to avoid bottlenecks.

◆ ② **Keep Subtasks Focused on Small, Actionable Steps**
■ If a subtask becomes too complex, consider **turning it into a separate task**.

◆ ③ **Use ClickUp Views for Better Visibility**
■ **List View:** Best for quick **task overviews**.
■ **Gantt View:** Best for **visualizing dependencies**.
■ **Board View:** Best for **Kanban-style workflows**.

◆ ④ **Combine Dependencies with Custom Fields**
■ Add **"Task Type"** fields to track dependencies across departments.
■ Use **"Risk Level"** to flag high-impact dependencies.

🚀 Final Thoughts: Creating Seamless Workflows with Dependencies and Subtasks

By effectively managing **Dependencies and Subtasks**, teams can:

■ **Improve project visibility** and eliminate bottlenecks.

■ **Ensure tasks follow the correct sequence** for smooth execution.

■ **Break down large deliverables** into manageable actions.

■ **Automate workflows** to save time and reduce errors.

In the next chapter, we'll explore **how to manage cross-team collaboration using Multi-Location Tasks in ClickUp**.

Multi-Location Tasks for Cross-Team Collaboration

In large-scale projects, multiple teams often need to work on the **same tasks but from different perspectives**. Traditional task management systems force duplication—creating the **same task in different spaces**, which leads to:

✖ **Confusion over which version is the latest**
✖ **Disjointed collaboration across departments**
✖ **Inefficient tracking of task progress**

ClickUp's **Multi-Location Tasks** solve this by allowing a **single task to exist in multiple locations**, ensuring all teams stay aligned while working on their respective responsibilities.

In this chapter, we'll explore:
◼ **What Multi-Location Tasks are and how they work**
◼ **How to set up and manage Multi-Location Tasks**
◼ **Use cases for different industries and teams**
◼ **Best practices for tracking progress without confusion**

📌 Understanding Multi-Location Tasks in ClickUp

Unlike traditional task duplication, ClickUp's Multi-Location feature allows a **single task** to appear in multiple Lists or Folders **without being copied**.

This means:
✔ **Changes made to a task reflect everywhere** instantly.
✔ **Multiple teams can track the same task** without working in silos.
✔ **Task updates, comments, and progress are centralized** in one place.

◆ **Example – A Marketing and Sales Team Collaboration:**
◼ The **Marketing Team** creates a landing page for a new product.
◼ The **Sales Team** needs visibility into the same task to align outreach.
◼ Instead of creating two separate tasks, the same task is added to both **Marketing** and **Sales** lists.

💡 **Best Practice: Use Multi-Location Tasks when a task requires input from multiple departments without duplication.**

📌 How to Create Multi-Location Tasks in ClickUp

Adding a task to multiple locations is **simple** and **intuitive**.

1 Assigning a Task to Multiple Locations

1 Open an existing **Task**.
2 Click on the **ellipsis menu (…)** in the top right corner.
3 Select **"Add to Another List"**.
4 Choose the **additional Lists or Folders** where the task should appear.

◼ Now, the task **exists in multiple places** without duplication.

📌 **Example – A Cross-Team Product Development Task**
✔ Task: *"Develop Product Feature X"*

✔ Primary List: **Engineering → Sprint Backlog**
✔ Additional List: **Marketing → Product Launch Plan**
✔ Additional List: **Customer Support → FAQ Documentation**

💡 **Best Practice:** Always ensure that **Multi-Location Tasks are assigned only where necessary** to avoid unnecessary clutter.

📌 Use Cases for Multi-Location Tasks

ClickUp's Multi-Location Tasks provide **cross-team visibility and efficiency**. Here are a few practical applications:

1️⃣ Product Development & Marketing Alignment

⬛ **Task:** "Launch Email Campaign for New Feature"
* Engineering → **Ensures product details are correct**
* Marketing → **Manages the email campaign**
* Sales → **Prepares customer outreach based on product release**

💡 **Best Practice:** Use **Task Custom Fields** to show different team responsibilities (e.g., "Marketing Owner" vs. "Engineering Contact").

2️⃣ Cross-Team Event Management

⬛ **Task:** "Plan Annual Company Summit"
* HR → **Handles logistics and scheduling**
* Marketing → **Manages event promotions**
* IT → **Sets up technical infrastructure**

💡 **Best Practice:** Add **Checklists** inside the task for each team's responsibilities.

3️⃣ IT and Operations Task Tracking

⬛ **Task:** "Upgrade CRM Software"
* IT Team → **Handles software updates**
* Operations → **Trains staff on new features**
* Finance → **Monitors budget for upgrades**

💡 **Best Practice:** Use **Custom Statuses** for tracking progress across different teams.

📌 Tracking Progress Without Confusion

Since a task appears in multiple Lists, it's **important to ensure clarity** in ownership and status updates.

4️⃣ Using Filters to View Multi-Location Tasks

ClickUp allows users to **filter tasks by location** to avoid overlap.

📌 **Steps to Filter Multi-Location Tasks:**
⬛ Open **List View**

■ Click **Filter** → **Location**
■ Select the **specific team's List**

♦ Best Practice: Save **Custom Views** so teams only see **tasks relevant to them**.

---

5 **Preventing Overlap with Custom Fields**

To differentiate **team responsibilities within a shared task**, use **Custom Fields** such as:
✔ **"Assigned Department"** → Marketing, Engineering, HR
✔ **"Task Owner"** → Individual responsible for updates
✔ **"Completion Phase"** → Ideation, Execution, Final Review

♦ Best Practice: Use **Tags** to flag tasks that span multiple teams, such as "Cross-Team" or "Multi-Department."

📌 **Best Practices for Using Multi-Location Tasks**

✔1 **Assign Ownership Clearly**
■ Each task should have a **primary owner** responsible for updates.
■ Use **@mentions in comments** to notify specific teams.

✔2 **Keep Task Statuses Consistent**
■ Ensure all teams use **consistent status updates** to avoid confusion.
■ Example: If "Completed" means different things for **IT vs. Marketing**, create a **Custom Status for each team**.

✔3 **Automate Status Changes for Multi-Team Workflows**
📌 **Example – Auto-Moving Tasks for Different Teams:**
■ **Trigger:** When Engineering marks "Feature X" as Complete
■ **Action:** Move task to "Marketing Review" in the Marketing List

✔4 **Use Dashboards to Track Multi-Location Tasks**
■ Create **Dashboard Widgets** for each department to track their portion of a shared task.
■ Use **Pie Charts or Progress Bars** to measure cross-team collaboration.

🚀 **Final Thoughts: Enhancing Cross-Team Collaboration with Multi-Location Tasks**

By implementing **Multi-Location Tasks effectively**, teams can:
■ **Eliminate task duplication and confusion**
■ **Improve transparency and collaboration across departments**
■ **Ensure alignment on shared tasks without losing ownership clarity**
■ **Track cross-functional work efficiently using ClickUp Views and Dashboards**

In the next chapter, we'll explore **how to build Custom Dashboards in ClickUp for real-time project insights**.

Custom Dashboards for Real-Time Insights

In complex projects, **real-time insights are essential** for decision-making, resource allocation, and progress tracking. Without a **centralized view**, teams often struggle with:

✖ Scattered project data across different locations
✖ Lack of visibility into team workloads
✖ Difficulty tracking key performance indicators (KPIs)
✖ Slow responses to bottlenecks and roadblocks

ClickUp's **Custom Dashboards** solve these challenges by allowing teams to **visualize critical data in one place**. Whether managing **task progress, workload distribution, budgets, or timelines**, Dashboards provide **real-time updates, reducing the need for manual reporting**.

In this chapter, we'll explore:
■ **What ClickUp Dashboards are and how they work**
■ **How to set up a Custom Dashboard**
■ **Key widgets for tracking project health**
■ **Best practices for designing dashboards based on team needs**

📌 Understanding ClickUp Dashboards

ClickUp Dashboards act as **a customizable project overview**, displaying data from multiple sources in **real-time**.

Key Benefits of ClickUp Dashboards:

✔ **Customizable Views** – Track only the data that matters to your team.
✔ **Real-Time Insights** – Monitor task progress and key project metrics instantly.
✔ **Multiple Widgets** – Use charts, tables, lists, and workload views to visualize performance.
✔ **Cross-Team Collaboration** – Share dashboards with stakeholders for transparency.

📌 Example – Using Dashboards to Manage a Marketing Campaign
■ **Task Overview** – Track campaign progress in a Pie Chart.
■ **Budget Tracking** – Use a Number Widget to monitor ad spend.
■ **Workload Distribution** – Ensure team members aren't overloaded.
■ **Timeline Visualization** – Use a Gantt Chart to see campaign milestones.

💡 **Best Practice: Customize dashboards based on the specific needs of different teams (e.g., executives, project managers, and developers may need different views).**

📌 How to Create a Custom Dashboard in ClickUp

1 Setting Up a New Dashboard

1 Navigate to **Dashboards** in the ClickUp sidebar.
2 Click **"+ New Dashboard"**.
3 Choose a **Dashboard Name** and adjust sharing settings.
4 Click **"Create"** to start customizing widgets.

📌 Example – Naming Your Dashboards for Clarity:
✔ **"Marketing Performance Dashboard"** – Tracks campaign KPIs.

✔ **"Development Sprint Dashboard"** – Monitors sprint progress.
✔ **"Executive Overview"** – Provides high-level company-wide insights.

💡 **Best Practice: Use clear naming conventions** so stakeholders can easily identify relevant dashboards.

📌 Essential Widgets for Tracking Project Health

ClickUp offers various **widgets** that provide different types of insights. Here's how to **choose the right ones** for your team.

Widget Type	Purpose	Example Use Case
Task List	Displays tasks from specific lists or spaces.	Show all overdue tasks.
Task Status Chart	Visualizes task progress across statuses.	Monitor how many tasks are in "In Progress" vs. "Completed."
Workload View	Shows task assignments by team member.	Ensure no team member is overloaded.
Time Tracking	Tracks hours logged per task or project.	View billable vs. non-billable hours.
Custom Chart (Pie, Bar, Line)	Provides data visualization for trends.	Track completed tasks per week.
Number Widget	Displays key metrics like budget, tickets resolved, or tasks completed.	Monitor ad spend or bug fixes.
Gantt Chart Widget	Shows project timelines and dependencies.	Track long-term planning and task relationships.

2 Adding Widgets to Your Dashboard

1 Click **"Add Widget"** in the Dashboard.
2 Select a **Widget Type** (e.g., Pie Chart, Workload, Custom Task List).
3 Configure the widget settings (choose **Lists, Spaces, or Folders** to pull data from).
4 Click **"Save"** and repeat for other widgets.

📌 **Example – Widgets for a Development Sprint Dashboard**
■ **Task Status Chart** – Tracks "To Do," "In Progress," "Blocked," "Done" tasks.
■ **Workload Widget** – Ensures balanced work among developers.
■ **Time Tracking Widget** – Measures effort logged per feature.
■ **Burndown Chart** – Shows progress toward sprint completion.

💡 **Best Practice: Avoid overcrowding dashboards. Use only the most relevant widgets for your team's needs.**

📌 Custom Dashboards for Different Teams

③ Executive Overview Dashboard (For Leadership & Stakeholders)

📌 **Purpose:** Provides **high-level project insights** without excessive details.

■ **Task Completion Rate (Pie Chart)** – Shows percentage of tasks completed.
■ **Budget vs. Actual Spending (Number Widget)** – Tracks project financials.
■ **Project Timeline (Gantt Chart)** – Displays major milestones.

💡 **Best Practice:** Keep **executive dashboards simple** with high-level summaries.

---

④ Project Manager Dashboard (For Day-to-Day Tracking)

📌 **Purpose:** Helps **project managers track workload, task progress, and deadlines**.

■ **Task List Widget** – Shows all open and overdue tasks.
■ **Workload Chart** – Balances task assignments among team members.
■ **Custom Bar Chart** – Tracks weekly productivity (tasks completed per person).

💡 **Best Practice:** Use **filters** to display only **relevant tasks** for easier navigation.

---

⑤ Agile Development Dashboard (For Software Teams)

📌 **Purpose:** Supports **scrum teams tracking sprints and development cycles**.

■ **Burndown Chart Widget** – Monitors sprint progress.
■ **Task Status Breakdown** – Shows backlog vs. active tasks.
■ **Time Tracking Widget** – Displays time spent per feature.

💡 **Best Practice:** Link dashboard widgets to **active sprint lists** for real-time tracking.

📌 Best Practices for Dashboard Optimization

• ① **Keep Dashboards Focused on Key Metrics**
✔ Avoid adding too many widgets—stick to **5-7 key insights per dashboard**.
✔ Ensure metrics are **actionable and relevant** for decision-making.

• ② **Regularly Review and Update Dashboards**
✔ Update dashboards **weekly or bi-weekly** to reflect **current project priorities**.
✔ Remove outdated widgets **to keep dashboards clean and relevant**.

• ③ **Share Dashboards with the Right Stakeholders**
✔ ClickUp allows **restricted access or full dashboard sharing**.
✔ Set dashboards to **View-Only** for external clients if needed.

• ④ **Use Automations to Keep Data Updated**
✔ ClickUp's **automations can update widgets** based on task status changes.
✔ Example: **Automatically move completed projects out of active view.**

🏁 Final Thoughts: Making Data-Driven Decisions with Custom Dashboards

By leveraging **Custom Dashboards**, teams can:

- **Gain real-time visibility** into project status and bottlenecks.
- **Track KPIs effectively** without manual reporting.
- **Improve collaboration and transparency** across departments.
- **Make data-driven decisions** to optimize project execution.

In the next chapter, we'll explore **how to track time and allocate resources effectively using ClickUp's built-in features**.

Time Tracking and Resource Allocation

Managing **complex projects efficiently** requires **tracking time spent on tasks** and ensuring **resources are allocated effectively**. Without a structured system for managing time and workload, teams face:

✘ **Missed deadlines due to poor time estimation**
✘ **Overworked team members and uneven workload distribution**
✘ **Budget overruns from underestimating resource needs**
✘ **Lack of data for optimizing future projects**

ClickUp provides **time tracking, workload management, and resource allocation tools** to help teams **improve efficiency, avoid burnout, and optimize project planning**.

In this chapter, we'll explore:
◼ **How ClickUp's Time Tracking works**
◼ **Setting up Workload and Resource Allocation in ClickUp**
◼ **Using Time Estimates for better planning**
◼ **Analyzing time tracking data to improve efficiency**

📌 Understanding ClickUp's Time Tracking Features

ClickUp offers **built-in time tracking**, allowing teams to:
✔ **Log time directly on tasks**
✔ **Track billable vs. non-billable hours**
✔ **Set time estimates for better workload planning**
✔ **Generate reports on time usage across projects**

 ◆ **Example – A Design Team Working on a Client Project:**
◼ **Task:** "Design Homepage UI"
◼ **Time Estimate:** 8 hours
◼ **Actual Time Logged:** 10 hours
◼ **Time Overrun:** 2 hours (25% over)

By comparing **estimated vs. actual time spent**, teams can **improve future planning and avoid delays**.

📌 How to Enable Time Tracking in ClickUp

1 Enabling Time Tracking for Your Workspace

1 Navigate to **Workspace Settings**.
2 Click on **Time Tracking**.
3 Toggle the switch to **Enable Time Tracking**.

2 Logging Time Manually or Automatically

✔ **Manual Entry:** Click on a task → Select **"Track Time"** → Enter hours worked.
✔ **Live Timer:** Click **"Start Timer"** to track time as you work.
✔ **Mobile & Desktop Apps:** Use ClickUp's **Chrome Extension or Mobile App** to log time on the go.

💡 **Best Practice: Encourage team members to use live tracking to capture actual work time accurately.**

📌 Using Time Estimates for Better Planning

ClickUp allows teams to **set time estimates** for tasks before work begins.

📌 How to Set Time Estimates on a Task:
1 Open a **Task**.
2 Click on **Time Estimate**.
3 Enter the **expected duration** (e.g., "5h" for 5 hours).

- **Example – Estimating a Software Development Sprint:**
■ **Task:** Develop API Integration → **Estimate: 12h**
■ **Task:** Conduct Code Review → **Estimate: 3h**
■ **Task:** QA Testing → **Estimate: 5h**

💡 **Best Practice: Review estimated vs. actual time spent** after each sprint to adjust estimates for future tasks.

📌 Setting Up Workload and Resource Allocation in ClickUp

ClickUp's **Workload View** helps teams distribute work evenly and **prevent burnout**.

3 Enabling Workload View

1 Click **"+ View"** in a List, Folder, or Space.
2 Select **"Workload"**.
3 Click **"Add View"**.

✔ Workload View **displays tasks assigned to each team member** and **their total time estimates**.
✔ Helps **spot overloaded team members** and **redistribute tasks** before burnout occurs.

📌 Example – Balancing Workload Across Team Members
👤 **Alice:** 40h planned → **Reduce load to 32h**
👤 **Bob:** 20h planned → **Assign additional 10h**
👤 **Chris:** 50h planned → **Reassign tasks to balance workload**

💡 **Best Practice: Adjust workloads weekly** to keep tasks evenly distributed.

📌 Tracking Billable vs. Non-Billable Hours

For teams working with **clients or budgets**, ClickUp supports **billable vs. non-billable tracking**.

📌 How to Track Billable Time:
1 Open a Task.
2 Click **"Track Time"**.
3 Select **Billable or Non-Billable**.

- **Example – Time Tracking for a Freelance Web Development Project:**
■ **Design Mockups** → 10 hours **(Billable)**
■ **Internal Team Meetings** → 5 hours **(Non-Billable)**
■ **Final Deployment** → 8 hours **(Billable)**

💡 **Best Practice: Use ClickUp's Reports to analyze how much of your time is billable vs. overhead work.**

📌 Generating Reports for Time Tracking & Resource Allocation

ClickUp provides **Time Tracking Reports** to analyze how time is spent across projects.

4 How to Access Time Tracking Reports

1 Navigate to **Dashboards**.
2 Click **"+ Add Widget"**.
3 Select **"Time Tracking Report"**.

📌 Example – Analyzing Time Usage Across Projects
■ **Project A:** 120h logged → 80% on development, 20% on meetings
■ **Project B:** 90h logged → 70% on coding, 30% on bug fixes

💡 **Best Practice: Use time reports to adjust team priorities and eliminate unnecessary overhead tasks.**

📌 Automating Time Tracking and Workload Adjustments

ClickUp's **Automations** can streamline time tracking and workload management.

📌 Example – Automatically Assigning Tasks Based on Available Capacity
■ **Trigger:** If a team member's weekly workload exceeds 40 hours
■ **Action:** Reassign excess tasks to available team members

📌 Example – Automating Reminders for Time Tracking
■ **Trigger:** If a task has no time logged after 3 days
■ **Action:** Send a reminder to log time

💡 **Best Practice: Automate workload balancing for a smoother team workflow.**

📌 Best Practices for Effective Time Tracking and Resource Allocation

- 1 **Establish Time Tracking Guidelines**
✔ Standardize how team members **log and track time**.
✔ Differentiate between **billable and non-billable hours**.

- 2 **Regularly Review Workload Distribution**
✔ Use **Workload View** to ensure no team members are overloaded.
✔ Reassign tasks if someone exceeds **40+ planned hours per week**.

- 3 **Compare Estimated vs. Actual Time Spent**
✔ Adjust **future time estimates** based on actual task completion data.
✔ Improve **forecasting for future sprints or projects**.

- 4 **Automate Time Tracking Where Possible**
✔ Use **ClickUp's timer** to reduce manual time entry errors.
✔ Set up **reminders** to prompt team members to log time daily.

🚀 Final Thoughts: Optimizing Productivity with Time Tracking & Resource Allocation

By leveraging **ClickUp's Time Tracking and Resource Allocation tools**, teams can:
- **Improve time estimation accuracy** and avoid missed deadlines.
- **Ensure fair workload distribution** across all team members.
- **Track billable vs. non-billable hours** for better financial planning.
- **Use reports and automation** to continuously optimize efficiency.

In the next chapter, we'll explore **how to align project goals with milestones in ClickUp for strategic execution**.

Integrating Goals with Project Milestones

Complex projects involve multiple teams, tasks, and dependencies. Without **clear alignment between goals and milestones**, teams can struggle with:

✖ **Lack of direction and purpose in daily tasks**
✖ **Inability to measure meaningful progress**
✖ **Missed deadlines due to untracked objectives**
✖ **Difficulty in communicating progress to stakeholders**

ClickUp's **Goals and Milestones** features ensure that **teams stay aligned with strategic objectives** while tracking key deliverables. By integrating **goals with milestones**, teams can:

◼ **Break down big-picture objectives into achievable steps**
◼ **Track progress in real-time to ensure targets are met**
◼ **Visualize dependencies between project milestones and tasks**
◼ **Improve accountability by linking milestones to key results**

In this chapter, we'll explore:
◼ **How ClickUp's Goals and Milestones Work**
◼ **How to Set and Align Goals in ClickUp**
◼ **Creating and Managing Milestones for Projects**
◼ **Best Practices for Tracking Goal Progress with Milestones**

📌 Understanding ClickUp's Goals & Milestones Features

ClickUp provides **two essential tools** for aligning strategy with execution:

1 **Goals:** High-level objectives that consist of measurable targets (Key Results).
2 **Milestones:** Critical checkpoints within a project that indicate significant progress.

Feature	Purpose	Example Use Case
Goals	Define long-term objectives	Increase customer retention by 20% in Q2
Milestones	Track major project progress points	"Website redesign 50% complete" by March 10

💡 **Best Practice: Use Goals to define what success looks like and Milestones to track major project deliverables.**

📌 How to Set and Align Goals in ClickUp

Goals in ClickUp are built with **Key Results** that define measurable progress.

1 Creating a Goal in ClickUp

1 Navigate to **Goals** in the ClickUp Sidebar.
2 Click **"Create Goal"**.
3 Define the **Goal Name** (e.g., "Launch New Marketing Website").
4 Set a **Due Date** for completion.

5 Add **Key Results** (metrics that measure progress toward the goal).
6 Assign **Owners** to ensure accountability.

📌 **Example – Goal: Improve Customer Satisfaction by 15%**
◼ **Key Result 1:** Reduce support response time from 24h to 6h.
◼ **Key Result 2:** Achieve an average customer rating of 4.8 stars.
◼ **Key Result 3:** Increase resolution rate from 85% to 95%.

💡 **Best Practice: Set SMART (Specific, Measurable, Achievable, Relevant, Time-bound) Goals to keep teams focused.**

📌 How to Create and Track Milestones in ClickUp

Milestones help teams track **major progress points within a project**.

2 Converting Tasks into Milestones

1 Open a **Task** in ClickUp.
2 Click the **three-dot menu (…)**.
3 Select **Convert to Milestone**.

Milestones appear in **Gantt Charts, Workload View, and Dashboards** to provide **clear tracking of key progress points**.

📌 **Example – Milestones for a Product Launch**
◼ **Milestone 1:** Finalize MVP Design (Feb 15)
◼ **Milestone 2:** Complete Beta Testing (March 10)
◼ **Milestone 3:** Launch Product (April 1)

💡 **Best Practice: Use Milestones to track high-impact deliverables rather than everyday tasks.**

📌 Aligning Goals with Project Milestones

Once Goals and Milestones are set, **link them together** to ensure alignment.

3 Connecting Milestones to Goals

📌 **How to Link Milestones to a Goal:**
1 Open the **Goal** section in ClickUp.
2 Click **"+ Add Target"** and choose **"Task"**.
3 Select **Milestones that contribute to the Goal**.

📌 **Example – Connecting Milestones to an Agile Sprint Goal**
◼ **Goal:** Deliver new homepage redesign.
• **Milestone 1:** Finalize UI mockups (Feb 15)
• **Milestone 2:** Implement front-end design (March 1)
• **Milestone 3:** Deploy live version (April 1)

💡 **Best Practice: Keep Goals high-level and Milestones specific to execution.**

📌 Tracking Goal Progress with ClickUp's Reporting Tools

ClickUp offers **Goal Dashboards and Progress Tracking Tools** to visualize how teams are advancing.

4 **Setting Up a Goal Tracking Dashboard**

1 Open **Dashboards**.
2 Click **"+ Add Widget"**.
3 Select **"Goal Progress"** to track completion %.
4 Add **"Milestone Tracking"** to monitor major project checkpoints.

📌 **Example – Tracking Q2 Marketing Goals**
■ **Goal Progress Widget:** 75% completed.
■ **Milestone Widget:** 3 out of 5 major campaign launches finished.

💡 **Best Practice: Review Goals and Milestones weekly to ensure on-time completion.**

📌 **Best Practices for Integrating Goals with Milestones**

✔ 1 **Define Goals Before Project Execution**
■ Start every major project with **a clear, measurable goal**.
■ Align project planning to **ensure milestones contribute to overall success**.

✔ 2 **Use Milestones for Major Checkpoints, Not Every Task**
■ Define only **critical project phases** as Milestones.
■ Avoid cluttering project views with unnecessary Milestones.

✔ 3 **Set Key Results that Directly Align with Milestones**
■ Each Milestone should **impact progress toward the goal**.
■ Use ClickUp's **Key Results feature** to track meaningful outcomes.

✔ 4 **Regularly Update Goal and Milestone Progress**
■ Assign **Owners** to ensure accountability.
■ Use **Automation** to trigger status updates based on task progress.

🚀 **Final Thoughts: Aligning Strategic Goals with Project Execution**

By integrating **Goals with Milestones**, teams can:
■ **Track progress toward major objectives efficiently.**
■ **Align daily work with strategic business goals.**
■ **Improve visibility into key project achievements.**
■ **Ensure stakeholder expectations are met with measurable results.**

In the next chapter, we'll explore **how to generate advanced reports in ClickUp for stakeholder updates and performance reviews.**

Advanced Reporting for Stakeholder Updates

Stakeholders, whether **executives, clients, or project sponsors**, require **clear, concise, and actionable reports** to track project progress and performance. Without a structured reporting process, teams risk:

✘ **Lack of transparency into project health**
✘ **Difficulty in tracking key performance metrics (KPIs)**
✘ **Misalignment between project execution and business goals**
✘ **Time-consuming manual reporting processes**

ClickUp offers **powerful reporting tools** that allow teams to:

■ **Generate real-time insights for stakeholders**
■ **Track key project performance indicators (KPIs)**
■ **Automate reporting to reduce manual work**
■ **Create visual dashboards for high-level overviews**

In this chapter, we'll explore:
■ **How to generate reports in ClickUp**
■ **Key reporting features for stakeholders**
■ **Automating stakeholder reports for efficiency**
■ **Best practices for delivering impactful reports**

📌 Understanding ClickUp's Reporting Capabilities

ClickUp provides **various reporting options** that cater to different stakeholder needs:

Reporting Feature	Purpose	Example Use Case
Dashboards	Visualize project status with charts & widgets	Executive-level project overviews
Workload Reports	Monitor team capacity and workload	Identify over/under-utilized team members
Time Tracking Reports	Track time spent on tasks and billable hours	Generate reports for client billing
Progress Reports	Measure completion percentage of tasks/milestones	Show progress of a product development sprint
Goal Reports	Monitor key objectives and key results (OKRs)	Track if marketing goals are on schedule
Task Reports	Analyze overdue, completed, or in-progress tasks	Identify blockers in a construction project

💡 **Best Practice: Choose the right reporting method based on stakeholder needs. Executives may prefer dashboards, while project managers require task reports.**

📌 How to Generate Reports in ClickUp

1 Creating a Custom Dashboard for Stakeholder Updates

1 Navigate to **Dashboards** in ClickUp.
2 Click **"+ New Dashboard"** and give it a relevant name (e.g., "Stakeholder Report – Q1").
3 Click **"+ Add Widget"** to customize your report.
4 Select widgets like:
✔ **Task Progress** – Tracks completed vs. pending tasks.
✔ **Milestone Tracker** – Displays major project checkpoints.
✔ **Goal Progress** – Measures how close the team is to achieving key objectives.
✔ **Burndown Chart** – Shows work remaining in a sprint.
5 Share the **Dashboard Link** with stakeholders or export it as a PDF.

📌 **Example – Dashboard for a Software Development Project:**
⬛ **Task Progress:** 75% of development completed
⬛ **Milestone Tracker:** Feature testing begins in 5 days
⬛ **Workload Chart:** Developers are at 90% capacity
⬛ **Goal Progress:** On track to launch MVP next month

💡 **Best Practice: Keep stakeholder dashboards simple with high-level insights. Avoid cluttering with unnecessary details.**

---

2 Exporting and Automating Reports

Stakeholders often prefer **weekly/monthly reports** via email. ClickUp allows teams to **automate report generation** to save time.

📌 **How to Export Reports in ClickUp:**
1 Navigate to a Dashboard or Task Report.
2 Click **"Export"** and select **CSV or PDF format**.
3 Send the report via email or upload it to a shared drive.

📌 **Automating Reports with Recurring Email Updates:**
⬛ Use **ClickUp Automations** to schedule email reports for stakeholders.
⬛ Example: **Every Friday at 10 AM, send a summary of completed tasks to executives.**

💡 **Best Practice: Automate recurring reports for consistency. Customize reports to highlight key insights, rather than sending raw data.**

📌 Key Reports for Different Stakeholders

3 Executive Summary Reports

📌 **Best For:** CEOs, Directors, Investors
✔ High-level project performance overview
✔ Financial metrics (budget vs. actual costs)
✔ Key risks and mitigation strategies

⬛ **Example Metrics to Include:**
✔ **Project Completion %** – How much of the project is done
✔ **Budget Spent vs. Remaining** – Financial tracking
✔ **Risks & Roadblocks** – Potential delays and mitigation plans

📍 **Best Practice: Use Pie Charts and Number Widgets for quick insights. Avoid detailed task-level updates.**

4️⃣ Project Progress Reports

📌 **Best For:** Project Managers, Department Heads
✔ Tracks overall progress against planned milestones
✔ Identifies blockers and bottlenecks
✔ Measures team performance

⬛ **Example Metrics to Include:**
✔ **Tasks Completed vs. Pending** – Work progress
✔ **Milestone Status** – If key deliverables are on track
✔ **Dependency Risks** – Tasks waiting on approvals

📍 **Best Practice: Use Gantt Charts and Burndown Charts to visualize progress over time.**

5️⃣ Team Performance & Workload Reports

📌 **Best For:** HR, Team Leads, Resource Managers
✔ Ensures even workload distribution
✔ Identifies overworked or underutilized employees
✔ Tracks efficiency of remote or hybrid teams

⬛ **Example Metrics to Include:**
✔ **Workload Balance** – Who is overloaded or under-assigned
✔ **Time Spent per Task** – Identify inefficiencies
✔ **Performance Metrics** – % of completed tasks per team member

📍 **Best Practice: Use Workload Reports to balance tasks and avoid burnout.**

6️⃣ Client or Customer-Facing Reports

📌 **Best For:** External Clients, Vendors
✔ Tracks deliverables for client projects
✔ Ensures transparency in outsourced work
✔ Provides billable vs. non-billable hours

⬛ **Example Metrics to Include:**
✔ **Deliverable Status** – Which client projects are on track
✔ **Time Spent on Client Work** – Hours logged by the team
✔ **Feedback Loops** – Pending client approvals

📍 **Best Practice: Use ClickUp's Time Tracking Reports for billable work transparency.**

📌 Best Practices for Effective Stakeholder Reporting

✔ 1️⃣ **Tailor Reports to the Audience**
⬛ Executives → Want **high-level summaries** (Dashboards).

■ Project Managers → Need **detailed task tracking** (Task Reports).
■ Clients → Require **clear deliverable updates** (PDF Exports).

✔2 **Keep Reports Visual and Concise**
■ Use **graphs, charts, and summary widgets** instead of text-heavy reports.
■ Highlight **only critical insights** to avoid overwhelming stakeholders.

✔3 **Automate Regular Updates**
■ Set up **weekly/monthly automated reports** via email or Slack.
■ Reduce **manual reporting effort** with ClickUp's scheduled exports.

✔4 **Track Progress in Real-Time**
■ Ensure reports are **updated dynamically** using ClickUp's live Dashboards.
■ Review **trends over time** rather than just current status snapshots.

🚀 **Final Thoughts: Streamlining Stakeholder Communication with Advanced Reporting**

By leveraging **ClickUp's reporting features**, teams can:
■ **Provide real-time insights to stakeholders with Dashboards**
■ **Reduce manual reporting work with automation**
■ **Track project milestones, team workload, and budget spend**
■ **Deliver clear and actionable updates for better decision-making**

In the next chapter, we'll explore **how to improve collaboration using ClickUp's real-time communication tools**.

Section 5:
Collaboration and Team Productivity

Real-Time Collaboration with Comments and Mentions

In complex projects, **efficient communication is key** to keeping tasks on track, aligning team members, and ensuring accountability. Without **real-time collaboration**, teams can face:

✘ Slow response times, leading to project delays
✘ Information silos where important details get lost
✘ Confusion over task ownership and next steps
✘ Missed critical updates due to scattered communication

ClickUp's **Comments and Mentions** enable teams to:

■ Communicate directly within tasks to provide context
■ Mention team members for quick responses and accountability
■ Attach files, share feedback, and resolve discussions efficiently
■ Reduce reliance on external emails and meetings

In this chapter, we'll explore:
■ How Comments and Mentions work in ClickUp
■ Best practices for keeping conversations structured
■ Using comments for approvals and feedback loops
■ Automating comment notifications for faster collaboration

📌 Understanding ClickUp's Comments and Mentions

ClickUp's **real-time commenting system** allows users to **leave feedback, discuss issues, and provide updates** directly within tasks, docs, and dashboards.

- **Key Features of ClickUp Comments:**
✔ **Threaded conversations** – Keep discussions organized within tasks
✔ **Mentions (@username, @team, @here, @everyone)** – Notify relevant people
✔ **Assign comments as action items** – Convert feedback into actionable tasks
✔ **React to comments with emojis** – Quickly acknowledge messages
✔ **Attach files and images** – Provide context without leaving ClickUp

📌 **Example – Using Comments in a Marketing Campaign Task:**
■ **Comment:** "@John Please upload the final version of the ad copy."
■ **Reply:** "Here it is! Let me know if any edits are needed. 📎 [Attached File]"
■ **Reaction:** 👍 (John reacts with a thumbs-up to acknowledge the update)

💡 Best Practice: Use mentions only when necessary to avoid notification overload.

📌 How to Use Mentions Effectively in ClickUp

ClickUp allows team members to mention **individuals, groups, or the entire workspace** to ensure messages reach the right people.

Mention Type	Purpose	Example Use Case
@username	Notify a specific person	"@Lisa Can you review this document?"
@team	Notify an entire team	"@Design Please confirm the new layout by Friday."
@here	Notify online members	"@here Quick update: Deadline moved to Monday!"
@everyone	Notify all workspace members	"@everyone Town hall meeting at 3 PM today."

💡 **Best Practice: Use @here for immediate attention and @team for team-wide updates without overwhelming everyone.**

📌 Using Comments for Approvals and Feedback Loops

ClickUp comments are useful for **review and approval workflows**, ensuring that all stakeholders provide input before moving forward.

📌 **Example – Requesting Approval on a Blog Post:**
■ **Comment:** "@Sarah Please approve this article for publishing."
■ **Reply:** "Looks great! Approved. ■"
■ **Next Step:** The task moves from "In Review" to "Published."

📌 **Example – Feedback Loop for a Design Team:**
■ **Comment:** "@Design Team The client wants a lighter color scheme."
■ **Reply:** "Understood! Here's an updated version. [Attached Image]"
■ **Follow-up Comment:** "@Marketing Does this align with the branding?"

💡 **Best Practice: Use comments to centralize feedback, reducing unnecessary meetings and emails.**

📌 Assigning Comments as Actionable Tasks

Instead of letting important feedback get lost in long comment threads, ClickUp allows users to **turn comments into action items**.

How to Assign a Comment as a Task

1. Hover over a comment.
2. Click the **"Assign"** button.
3. Select the **team member responsible**.
4. The comment now becomes an **assigned action item** within the task.

📌 **Example – Assigning a Comment as a Task for a Social Media Team:**
■ **Comment:** "@Emma Please update the Instagram caption for better engagement."
■ **Action:** Convert this comment into a **subtask with a deadline**.

💡 **Best Practice: Use assigned comments to ensure accountability and prevent task-related discussions from being forgotten.**

📌 Using ClickUp's Comment Automations for Faster Collaboration

ClickUp allows teams to **automate comment notifications** and task updates, ensuring that **key stakeholders are informed without manual effort**.

How to Set Up Comment Automations

1. Navigate to **Automation Settings**.
2. Choose **"When a Comment is Added"** as a trigger.
3. Select an action (e.g., **Notify Assignee, Change Task Status, or Assign a Task**).

📌 **Example – Automating Comment-Based Task Updates**
◼ **Trigger:** When a comment contains the word **"Approved"**
◼ **Action:** Move the task to **"Final Review"**

📌 **Example – Automating Notifications for Mentions**
◼ **Trigger:** When a comment mentions **@Marketing Team**
◼ **Action:** Send a Slack notification to the marketing channel

💡 **Best Practice: Use automations to reduce manual follow-ups and streamline workflows.**

📌 Best Practices for Real-Time Collaboration with Comments & Mentions

✔1 **Keep Conversations Focused**
◼ Use **threaded replies** to maintain context.
◼ Avoid **off-topic discussions** within tasks—use ClickUp Chat for casual updates.

✔2 **Use Mentions Wisely**
◼ Tag only relevant people to **avoid notification overload**.
◼ Use **@team instead of @everyone** to target updates efficiently.

✔3 **Convert Important Comments into Actionable Tasks**
◼ Assign comments **with clear ownership and deadlines**.
◼ Use **task status changes** to reflect approval decisions.

✔4 **Automate Notifications to Reduce Manual Work**
◼ Use **ClickUp Automations** to send Slack/email updates when key comments are added.
◼ Set up **reminders for unanswered comments** to prevent bottlenecks.

🚀 Final Thoughts: Enhancing Team Productivity with Real-Time Collaboration

By effectively using **ClickUp's Comments and Mentions**, teams can:
◼ **Ensure real-time communication within tasks**
◼ **Reduce email clutter and streamline discussions**
◼ **Improve accountability with assigned comments**
◼ **Speed up approvals and feedback loops**

In the next chapter, we'll explore **how to assign roles and permissions strategically in ClickUp to enhance security and team productivity**.

Assigning Roles and Permissions Strategically

Effective collaboration in **complex projects** depends on **clear role assignments and structured permissions**. Without a well-defined system, teams may experience:

✗ **Unauthorized access to sensitive information**
✗ **Confusion over task ownership and decision-making**
✗ **Accidental modifications or deletions**
✗ **Inefficiencies due to lack of role clarity**

ClickUp provides a **flexible role-based permission system** that allows teams to:

■ **Control access to tasks, lists, and workspaces**
■ **Ensure accountability with clear role assignments**
■ **Maintain data security by restricting modifications**
■ **Improve efficiency by defining user responsibilities**

In this chapter, we'll cover:
■ **Understanding roles and permissions in ClickUp**
■ **How to assign roles effectively**
■ **Using custom permissions for secure collaboration**
■ **Best practices for managing access levels**

📌 Understanding ClickUp Roles and Permissions

ClickUp offers **hierarchical role-based access control**, ensuring team members only have access to **what they need**.

Role	Access Level	Best Use Case
Owner	Full control over all settings, permissions, and billing.	Company leadership or IT administrators.
Admin	Manage users, permissions, and workspace settings.	Project managers or department leads.
Member	Standard team members with task and project access.	Employees or regular contributors.
Guest	Limited access, view-only or comment access.	Clients, external vendors, or freelancers.
Viewer	Read-only access with no editing privileges.	Stakeholders who only need updates.

📌 **Example – Assigning Roles in a Marketing Project:**
■ **Owner:** CEO (Full workspace control)
■ **Admin:** Marketing Manager (Manages team roles and access)
■ **Member:** Content Writers & Designers (Create and edit tasks)
■ **Guest:** External Ad Agency (View & comment on campaigns)

💡 **Best Practice: Keep admin roles limited to avoid unnecessary modifications.**

📌 How to Assign Roles in ClickUp

1️⃣ Assigning User Roles in a Workspace

1️⃣ Go to **Workspace Settings → People**.
2️⃣ Select a team member.
3️⃣ Click **"Change Role"** and assign **Owner, Admin, Member, or Guest**.

📌 Example – Setting Up Roles in a Software Development Team:
✔ **Owner:** CTO – Oversees all projects.
✔ **Admin:** Project Manager – Controls team access.
✔ **Member:** Developers – Manage sprint tasks.
✔ **Guest:** QA Consultant – Reviews test cases but can't modify them.

💡 **Best Practice: Review role assignments quarterly to ensure security.**

📌 Using Custom Permissions for Secure Collaboration

ClickUp allows **fine-grained control** over who can **edit, delete, and view specific items**.

2️⃣ Setting Custom Permissions for Folders, Lists, and Tasks

1️⃣ Navigate to a **Folder, List, or Task**.
2️⃣ Click **"Share"** and select **Permissions**.
3️⃣ Choose from:
✔ **Full Access** – Can edit, delete, and modify tasks.
✔ **Can Edit** – Can modify but not delete tasks.
✔ **Can Comment** – Can leave feedback but not edit.
✔ **Can View** – Read-only access.

📌 Example – Permission Setup for a Client-Facing Project:
✔ **Project Manager** – Full access to edit all deliverables.
✔ **Copywriter & Designer** – Can edit assigned tasks only.
✔ **Client (Guest)** – Can view and comment but not modify.

💡 **Best Practice: Limit delete permissions to admins to avoid accidental data loss.**

📌 Managing Permissions for Private and Public Projects

ClickUp allows users to **restrict access at different levels** to protect sensitive data.

3️⃣ Creating Private vs. Public Projects

⬛ **Private Projects:** Visible only to invited users (e.g., confidential R&D projects).
⬛ **Public Projects:** Accessible to all members of the workspace (e.g., company-wide announcements).

📌 Example – Using Private Projects for HR & Finance Teams:
✔ **HR Documents:** Only HR admins can access.
✔ **Salary Review Tasks:** Restricted to finance executives.
✔ **Company News:** Public to all team members.

💡 **Best Practice: Use private projects for sensitive data like HR, finance, and legal tasks.**

📌 Best Practices for Managing Roles & Permissions

✔1 Assign Roles Based on Need, Not Title
■ Ensure **only essential team members have admin access**.
■ Give **external collaborators guest access** instead of full membership.

✔2 Regularly Audit User Roles
■ Conduct **quarterly reviews** to update roles and remove inactive users.
■ Limit **Owner and Admin roles** to prevent unnecessary settings changes.

✔3 Use Task-Level Permissions for Confidential Work
■ Restrict **who can modify critical documents and sensitive data**.
■ Assign **comment-only access** for review tasks.

✔4 Automate Permissions for Efficiency
■ Set up **default role-based permissions** for new hires.
■ Use ClickUp's **Automations to adjust access** based on task status.

🚀 Final Thoughts: Enhancing Security & Collaboration with Strategic Roles

By setting up **clear roles and permissions**, teams can:
■ **Enhance security while improving collaboration**
■ **Prevent accidental modifications or data loss**
■ **Ensure each team member has the right level of access**
■ **Simplify stakeholder involvement without overloading them**

In the next chapter, we'll explore **how to use ClickUp Chat for seamless team communication**.

Using ClickUp Chat for Seamless Communication

Effective communication is the **foundation of successful project management**, especially in complex workflows where multiple teams, tasks, and deadlines intersect. Without an **organized communication system**, teams often experience:

✗ **Misalignment between departments and stakeholders**
✗ **Lost or scattered information across multiple platforms**
✗ **Inefficient workflows due to delayed responses**
✗ **Over-reliance on emails, leading to slow decision-making**

ClickUp **Chat View** centralizes communication, ensuring that teams can:

■ **Discuss projects without switching between apps**
■ **Keep communication organized within the workspace**
■ **Mention team members for immediate attention**
■ **Reduce email clutter and speed up decision-making**

In this chapter, we'll cover:
■ **What ClickUp Chat View is and how it works**
■ **Setting up Chat View for different team needs**
■ **Best practices for keeping communication organized**
■ **Integrating ClickUp Chat with tasks and notifications**

📌 Understanding ClickUp Chat View

ClickUp **Chat View** provides a **real-time messaging system** directly within your workspace, allowing teams to **communicate without leaving ClickUp**.

- **Key Features of ClickUp Chat:**
✔ **Real-time messaging** – Quick, seamless team discussions
✔ **Threaded conversations** – Keep discussions focused on topics
✔ **Mentions (@username, @team, @here, @everyone)** – Notify relevant team members
✔ **File attachments** – Share documents, images, and links directly
✔ **Integrations** – Sync conversations with Slack, Email, and ClickUp tasks

📌 **Example – A Marketing Team Using ClickUp Chat:**
■ **Campaign Chat:** Discussing social media ad strategies
■ **Product Launch Chat:** Sharing assets between designers and content teams
■ **HR Team Chat:** Keeping internal discussions within ClickUp instead of email

💡 **Best Practice: Use dedicated Chat Views for different teams or projects to keep discussions structured.**

📌 How to Set Up Chat View in ClickUp

1 Adding a Chat View to a Space, Folder, or List

1. Open ClickUp and navigate to a **Space, Folder, or List**.
2. Click **"+ View"** at the top.
3. Select **"Chat"** and click **"Add View"**.

4 Name the chat (e.g., "Development Team Chat" or "Client Feedback").
5 Start messaging!

📌 **Example – Setting Up ClickUp Chat for an Agile Development Team:**
✔ **Sprint Chat:** Discuss weekly development tasks
✔ **Bug Fix Chat:** Report issues and assign fixes in real time
✔ **Release Planning Chat:** Align engineers, designers, and product managers

💡 **Best Practice: Pin important messages at the top of Chat View to ensure key updates remain visible.**

📌 Best Practices for Organizing Team Communication in ClickUp Chat

To keep conversations **clear and efficient**, follow these best practices:

✔ 1 **Use Threaded Messages for Focused Conversations**
■ Avoid long message chains by replying to specific comments in **threads**.
■ Example: A designer asks for feedback – teammates respond in the same thread instead of sending new messages.

✔ 2 **Use Mentions to Notify the Right People**
■ **@username** → Notifies a specific individual.
■ **@team** → Alerts the entire team for major updates.
■ **@here** → Notifies only online members.
■ **@everyone** → Alerts all members, regardless of availability.

📌 **Example – Notifying a Design Team:**
■ "@DesignTeam Can we finalize the homepage mockup by Friday?"

💡 **Best Practice: Use @here sparingly to avoid unnecessary distractions.**

✔ 3 **Attach Files & Screenshots for Context**
■ Instead of typing long explanations, attach **designs, reports, and screenshots** directly in ClickUp Chat.

📌 **Example – A Developer Sharing a Bug Report:**
■ "This issue appears on mobile. See attached screenshot."

💡 **Best Practice: Use file attachments to make discussions more actionable and reduce confusion.**

✔ 4 **Convert Messages into Tasks for Actionable Items**
■ ClickUp allows you to **turn a chat message into a task** for easy follow-ups.

How to Convert a Chat Message into a Task:

1 Hover over a message in Chat View.
2 Click **"… More Options"**.
3 Select **"Convert to Task"**.
4 Assign it to a team member and set a due date.

📌 **Example – A Marketing Manager Creating a Task from a Chat:**
■ **Message:** "We need to update the ad copy for Q2 campaigns."
■ **Converted Task:** "Revise Facebook & Instagram Ads – Due: March 15."

💡 Best Practice: Convert chat messages into tasks whenever an action is required to ensure follow-through.

📌 Integrating ClickUp Chat with Notifications & Other Tools

ClickUp Chat integrates with **other collaboration tools**, reducing the need for external messaging apps.

5 Syncing ClickUp Chat with Slack & Email

■ **Slack Integration:** Send ClickUp messages directly to Slack channels.
■ **Email Integration:** Forward ClickUp Chat messages to email for external stakeholders.

📌 Example – Using ClickUp Chat & Slack for Remote Teams:
✔ ClickUp Chat → Internal team discussions & task updates
✔ Slack → Quick external client communication

💡 Best Practice: Use ClickUp Chat for structured project communication and Slack for informal discussions.

📌 How ClickUp Chat Improves Cross-Team Communication

ClickUp Chat is **useful for multiple teams**, keeping discussions centralized while allowing structured workflows.

6 Use Cases for Different Teams

Team	How They Use ClickUp Chat	Example
Marketing	Campaign discussions, content approvals	"Can we finalize the email sequence today?"
Development	Bug tracking, sprint discussions	"This issue affects the checkout flow. Fixing now."
HR & Admin	Internal policy updates, recruitment planning	"Reminder: Team meeting tomorrow at 2 PM."
Client Support	Customer feedback, issue resolution	"Customer reported a payment issue. Investigating."

💡 Best Practice: Create different Chat Views for different teams to maintain clear, structured discussions.

📌 Best Practices for Effective ClickUp Chat Usage

✔ 1 Create Dedicated Chat Views for Each Team or Project
■ Example: "Design Team Chat," "Client Feedback Chat," "QA Testing Chat."

✔ 2 Keep Messages Focused & Actionable
■ Use **clear, concise updates** instead of long messages.
■ Example: Instead of "Hey, can you check this?" → "@Mike Can you review the homepage design before 5 PM?"

✔3 **Reduce Redundant Notifications**
◼ Avoid overusing @everyone mentions.
◼ Set **notification preferences** to prevent distractions.

✔4 **Convert Important Discussions into Tasks**
◼ If a message requires action, **convert it into a task with due dates**.

✔5 **Use ClickUp Automations for Smarter Notifications**
◼ Example: **Auto-send a message in Chat View when a new high-priority task is added.**

🚀 **Final Thoughts: Boosting Team Productivity with ClickUp Chat**

By leveraging **ClickUp Chat**, teams can:
◼ **Reduce the need for scattered emails & external messaging apps**
◼ **Ensure real-time, structured communication in the workspace**
◼ **Streamline discussions with threaded replies, mentions, and task conversions**
◼ **Integrate chat with Slack, Email, and ClickUp notifications for seamless collaboration**

In the next chapter, we'll explore **how to use Feedback Loops and Iterative Workflows in ClickUp to improve project quality and efficiency.**

Feedback Loops and Iterative Workflows

In complex projects, **continuous improvement is essential** for delivering high-quality results. Without an effective **feedback loop**, teams may face:

✗ Delayed problem detection leading to project bottlenecks
✗ Missed opportunities for refinement and improvement
✗ Stakeholder dissatisfaction due to misalignment
✗ Lack of agility in adjusting to new requirements

ClickUp provides robust tools to support **feedback loops and iterative workflows**, ensuring that:

■ Teams receive timely feedback on tasks and deliverables
■ Workflows evolve based on insights and changing priorities
■ Stakeholders remain engaged through structured review processes
■ Projects improve over time by leveraging data-driven decisions

In this chapter, we'll cover:
■ Understanding Feedback Loops and Their Importance
■ How to Set Up Iterative Workflows in ClickUp
■ Using Comments, Approvals, and Automations for Feedback
■ Best Practices for Implementing Continuous Improvement

📌 Understanding Feedback Loops and Their Importance

A **feedback loop** is a **systematic process of gathering, reviewing, and acting upon feedback** to improve performance.

- **Types of Feedback Loops in Project Management:**
✔ **Internal Team Feedback** – Developers, designers, and managers reviewing work collaboratively.
✔ **Client/Stakeholder Feedback** – Customers or executives providing insights on deliverables.
✔ **User Feedback** – Product teams iterating based on customer responses.

📌 **Example – Feedback Loop in a Software Development Project:**
■ **Step 1:** A developer submits code for review.
■ **Step 2:** The project manager and QA team provide comments.
■ **Step 3:** The developer refines the code based on the feedback.
■ **Step 4:** The improved code is merged into production.
■ **Step 5:** Users provide feedback, initiating another improvement cycle.

💡 **Best Practice: Ensure that feedback is actionable and linked to specific tasks for easy implementation.**

📌 How to Set Up Iterative Workflows in ClickUp

An **iterative workflow** follows a **cycle of execution, review, refinement, and re-execution** to improve outputs over time.

1 Designing an Iterative Workflow in ClickUp

1 **Create a List** for your project or deliverable (e.g., "Product Enhancements").
2 **Define Stages** using ClickUp **Statuses** (e.g., "Draft" → "Review" → "Feedback" → "Final Approval" →

"Completed").

3 Assign **task owners** for each phase.

4 Use **recurring tasks** for ongoing reviews.

5 Set up **automations** to notify stakeholders when feedback is needed.

📌 **Example – Iterative Workflow for a Marketing Team:**

✔ **Draft Stage:** Content writers create blog posts.

✔ **Review Stage:** Editors provide feedback and request revisions.

✔ **Approval Stage:** Marketing leads approve final content.

✔ **Publish Stage:** The content is scheduled for release.

✔ **Analyze & Improve:** Performance data is reviewed, leading to refinements.

💡 **Best Practice: Use ClickUp's Custom Statuses to define iterative cycles clearly.**

📌 Using Comments, Approvals, and Automations for Feedback

ClickUp enables **structured feedback** through comments, approvals, and automation.

2 Gathering Feedback Using Task Comments

✔ **Mention stakeholders (@username) to request input.**

✔ **Attach files or screenshots for detailed feedback.**

✔ **Use threaded comments to keep discussions organized.**

📌 **Example – Design Team Feedback Process:**

⬛ **Designer:** "@MarketingTeam Here's the homepage redesign. Thoughts?"

⬛ **Marketing Lead:** "Looks great! Can we adjust the color scheme slightly?"

⬛ **Designer:** "Updated the colors. Let me know if this works."

💡 **Best Practice: Pin key comments for easy reference throughout the review process.**

---

3 Using ClickUp's Approvals Feature

Approvals allow teams to **formalize feedback processes** and ensure stakeholders sign off on work before proceeding.

📌 **How to Enable Approvals in ClickUp:**

1 Open a task.

2 Click **"Add Custom Field"** → Select **"Approval"**.

3 Assign an approver (e.g., project manager, client).

4 The approver selects **"Approved" or "Changes Needed."**

📌 **Example – Using Approvals in a Client Project:**

⬛ **Task:** Website mockup ready for review.

⬛ **Client Approval Field:** "Waiting for Approval" → "Approved!"

⬛ **Next Step:** Move the task to the "Development" phase.

💡 **Best Practice: Use Approvals to eliminate ambiguity in finalizing deliverables.**

---

4 Automating Feedback Requests

ClickUp **Automations** ensure feedback is requested at the right time without manual follow-ups.

📌 **How to Automate Feedback Loops in ClickUp:**

⬛ **Trigger:** Task moves to "Needs Review" status.

⬛ **Action:** Automatically assign the task to the reviewer and send a comment: "@Reviewer Please review and provide feedback."

📌 **Example – Automating Feedback in a Video Production Project:**

✔ **Trigger:** When a video edit is ready.

✔ **Action:** Notify the creative director and assign a review task.

✔ **Outcome:** Feedback is gathered without delays, ensuring a smooth revision process.

💡 **Best Practice: Set up automations for repetitive feedback requests to avoid delays.**

📌 **Best Practices for Implementing Continuous Improvement**

✔1 **Establish Clear Feedback Guidelines**

⬛ Define how and when feedback should be provided.

⬛ Encourage **constructive feedback** with specific action points.

✔2 **Use Data to Inform Iterations**

⬛ Leverage **Dashboards and Reports** to track the impact of feedback-driven improvements.

⬛ Example: If marketing conversion rates improve after content changes, note those best practices.

✔3 **Keep Feedback Cycles Efficient**

⬛ Avoid **long delays** between feedback and implementation.

⬛ Use ClickUp's **reminder notifications** to ensure follow-ups happen.

✔4 **Maintain a Centralized Record of Feedback**

⬛ Store all feedback **within ClickUp tasks** instead of scattered emails.

⬛ Use **Task History** to track previous revisions and improvements.

✔5 **Encourage a Culture of Continuous Improvement**

⬛ Foster an **open environment** where feedback is welcomed, not feared.

⬛ Align feedback with **team and company goals** to show its value.

🚀 **Final Thoughts: Driving Success with Feedback Loops and Iterative Workflows**

By implementing **feedback loops and iterative workflows**, teams can:

⬛ **Deliver higher-quality work through continuous refinements.**

⬛ **Improve collaboration and efficiency by centralizing feedback in ClickUp.**

⬛ **Ensure structured approvals and revisions without delays.**

⬛ **Leverage automation to streamline repetitive feedback tasks.**

In the next chapter, we'll explore **how to integrate ClickUp with Slack, Google Drive, and Zoom for seamless external collaboration.**

Section 6:
Integrations and Extensions

Connecting ClickUp with Slack, Google Drive, and Zoom

Managing **complex projects** requires seamless communication, document sharing, and efficient collaboration across multiple platforms. Without proper integration, teams often struggle with:

✘ **Scattered information across different apps**
✘ **Time wasted switching between tools**
✘ **Missed updates and lost communication threads**
✘ **Lack of visibility into project discussions and shared files**

By integrating ClickUp with **Slack, Google Drive, and Zoom**, teams can:

▪ **Streamline real-time communication without leaving ClickUp**
▪ **Store and access important documents directly from tasks**
▪ **Schedule and track meetings efficiently within the workspace**
▪ **Reduce tool fatigue and keep workflows centralized**

In this chapter, we'll cover:
▪ **How ClickUp integrates with Slack for real-time messaging**
▪ **How to connect ClickUp with Google Drive for document storage**
▪ **Using Zoom integration for seamless meeting management**
▪ **Best practices for optimizing cross-tool collaboration**

📌 Integrating ClickUp with Slack for Instant Communication

Slack is a widely used communication tool for **instant messaging, team discussions, and notifications**. The **ClickUp-Slack integration** allows teams to:

✔ **Create ClickUp tasks directly from Slack messages**
✔ **Receive real-time ClickUp notifications in Slack channels**
✔ **Update task statuses without leaving Slack**
✔ **Automatically sync important updates between Slack and ClickUp**

🔗 How to Set Up the ClickUp-Slack Integration

1. **Go to ClickUp Settings** → Navigate to **Integrations**.
2. Select **Slack** and click **Connect**.
3. Authorize ClickUp to access your Slack workspace.
4. Choose which **Slack channels** will receive ClickUp notifications.
5. Configure **notifications** based on task activity (e.g., new tasks, status updates, due dates).

📌 **Example – A Development Team Using ClickUp & Slack:**
◼ **New Bug Report:** A user reports a bug in Slack → The team creates a ClickUp task directly from the Slack message.
◼ **Task Status Updates:** Whenever a bug is fixed, ClickUp automatically posts an update in Slack.

💡 **Best Practice: Set up a dedicated Slack channel for ClickUp updates to avoid unnecessary notifications in general discussions.**

◼ **Using ClickUp's Slack Commands**

ClickUp allows teams to execute **task actions directly within Slack** using slash commands:

Command	Action
`/clickup new`	Create a new ClickUp task from Slack
`/clickup find [task name]`	Search for a task in ClickUp
`/clickup link [task URL]`	Link a task to a Slack message
`/clickup status`	View a task's current status

📌 **Example – Quickly Creating a Task in Slack:**
◼ A marketing manager messages the team: "We need a landing page update."
◼ Instead of switching to ClickUp, they type: `/clickup new Landing Page Update – Due Friday.`
◼ The task is automatically added to ClickUp.

💡 **Best Practice: Use `/clickup` new to instantly convert Slack discussions into actionable tasks.**

📌 **Connecting ClickUp with Google Drive for Document Management**

Google Drive is essential for **document collaboration, file storage, and easy access to shared assets**. Integrating ClickUp with Google Drive enables teams to:

✔ **Attach Google Docs, Sheets, and Slides directly to ClickUp tasks**
✔ **Preview and edit Google Drive files without leaving ClickUp**
✔ **Search for Google Drive files within ClickUp**
✔ **Automatically create folders for new projects**

🔗 **How to Set Up the ClickUp-Google Drive Integration**

1️⃣ Go to ClickUp **Settings** → Select **Integrations**.
2️⃣ Click **Google Drive** and choose **Connect Account**.
3️⃣ Authorize ClickUp to access Google Drive.
4️⃣ Open a task in ClickUp → Click **Attach** → Select **Google Drive File**.
5️⃣ Search for and attach relevant documents.

📌 **Example – A Marketing Team Managing Blog Content:**
◼ **Task:** "Write Q1 Content Calendar."

■ **Attached File:** A Google Sheet tracking topics and deadlines.
■ **Workflow:** Team members edit the sheet directly from ClickUp, ensuring updates are centralized.

💡 **Best Practice: Use ClickUp Folders to organize Google Drive links for easy access to project-related files.**

■ Organizing Google Drive Files in ClickUp

To keep files organized, teams can:

✔ **Create a dedicated ClickUp Folder for each project and link Google Drive files**
✔ **Use Google Drive's shared permissions to control access**
✔ **Rename files consistently to match project phases**

📌 **Example – Organizing Google Drive Files for a Product Launch:**
📂 **Product Launch Folder (ClickUp)** → Contains Google Docs for:
■ **Marketing Plan**
■ **Launch Checklist**
■ **Budget & Expenses**

💡 **Best Practice: Use ClickUp's file previews to check Google Drive docs without switching tabs.**

📌 Using ClickUp's Zoom Integration for Meeting Management

ClickUp's **Zoom integration** streamlines video calls by:

✔ **Scheduling Zoom meetings directly from ClickUp tasks**
✔ **Linking Zoom recordings to relevant tasks**
✔ **Tracking meeting notes within ClickUp Docs**

🔗 How to Set Up the ClickUp-Zoom Integration

1️⃣ **Go to ClickUp Settings** → Select **Integrations**.
2️⃣ Click **Zoom** and connect your Zoom account.
3️⃣ When creating a task, click **Attach Zoom Meeting**.
4️⃣ ClickUp will generate a **Zoom link** within the task description.
5️⃣ After the meeting, the **recording is automatically linked** to the task.

📌 **Example – An Engineering Team Using ClickUp & Zoom for Sprint Reviews:**
■ **Task:** "Sprint Planning Meeting" – Linked to a scheduled Zoom call.
■ **Meeting Notes:** Added to ClickUp Docs.
■ **Zoom Recording:** Automatically saved in ClickUp for later reference.

💡 **Best Practice: Record Zoom meetings and link them to ClickUp tasks for team members who couldn't attend.**

📌 Best Practices for Optimizing Cross-Tool Collaboration

✔1 Automate Notifications to Reduce Manual Updates
■ Set **ClickUp-Slack notifications** for key task updates.
■ Example: When a new task is assigned, send a Slack notification.

✔2 Centralize Document Management with Google Drive
■ Attach all key documents to ClickUp tasks to **avoid searching in multiple places**.
■ Example: Instead of sharing links in emails, store them within ClickUp tasks.

✔3 Use Zoom for Quick Decision-Making
■ Schedule **recurring Zoom meetings** within ClickUp for ongoing projects.
■ Example: Weekly stand-up meetings linked to ClickUp tasks.

✔4 Ensure Proper Access Permissions Across Tools
■ Restrict **Google Drive document editing** based on team roles.
■ Limit **ClickUp guest access** for external collaborators.

✔5 Keep Integrations Simple and Relevant
■ Only connect **Slack channels that need ClickUp updates**.
■ Limit Google Drive file attachments **to avoid clutter in ClickUp tasks**.

🚀 Final Thoughts: Enhancing Productivity with ClickUp Integrations

By integrating ClickUp with **Slack, Google Drive, and Zoom**, teams can:
■ **Reduce time spent switching between apps**
■ **Streamline task communication and notifications**
■ **Centralize document sharing for easy access**
■ **Enhance meeting management with Zoom-linked tasks**

In the next chapter, we'll explore **how to leverage ClickUp's API for custom automation and solutions**.

Leveraging ClickUp API for Custom Solutions

ClickUp offers a powerful **Application Programming Interface (API)** that allows teams to **build custom solutions, automate tasks, and integrate with other tools** beyond its built-in integrations. By leveraging the ClickUp API, teams can:

■ **Automate repetitive actions to save time**
■ **Customize workflows beyond default ClickUp features**
■ **Integrate with proprietary or third-party applications**
■ **Extract, analyze, and visualize data for reporting**

Without an API-driven approach, teams may struggle with:

✘ **Limited automation leading to manual inefficiencies**
✘ **Siloed systems with disconnected tools**
✘ **Lack of flexibility in customizing ClickUp for unique use cases**

In this chapter, we'll explore:
■ **What the ClickUp API is and how it works**
■ **How to generate an API key and authenticate requests**
■ **Common use cases for leveraging ClickUp's API**
■ **Best practices for implementing custom integrations**

📌 Understanding the ClickUp API

The **ClickUp API** is a RESTful API that enables developers to interact with ClickUp programmatically. It allows users to:

✔ **Retrieve, update, and create tasks automatically**
✔ **Manage spaces, lists, and folders programmatically**
✔ **Fetch reports and track progress via external dashboards**
✔ **Sync ClickUp with third-party tools like CRMs, ERPs, or proprietary databases**

🔗 Getting Started: How to Generate an API Key

To use the ClickUp API, you first need to generate an **API key**:

1️⃣ **Go to ClickUp Settings** → Navigate to **Apps**.
2️⃣ Select **ClickUp API**.
3️⃣ Click **Generate API Key** and copy the key.
4️⃣ Use the API key in requests to authenticate your application.

📌 Example – Using an API Key in a Request:
To retrieve all tasks from a specific ClickUp List:

```
curl -X GET "https://api.clickup.com/api/v2/list/{LIST_ID}/task" \
  -H "Authorization: {YOUR_API_KEY}" \
  -H "Content-Type: application/json"
```

💡 **Best Practice: Store API keys securely in environment variables instead of hardcoding them in scripts.**

📌 Common Use Cases for ClickUp API

1️⃣ Automating Task Creation from External Apps

Automatically create ClickUp tasks when an event occurs in another system (e.g., a support ticket is submitted in a CRM).

📌 Example – Auto-Create a Task in ClickUp When a New Support Ticket is Logged:

```python
import requests

api_key = "YOUR_API_KEY"
list_id = "123456789"
url = f"https://api.clickup.com/api/v2/list/{list_id}/task"

headers = {
    "Authorization": api_key,
    "Content-Type": "application/json"
}

data = {
    "name": "New Support Ticket",
    "description": "Customer reported an issue. Needs review.",
    "status": "Open"
}

response = requests.post(url, json=data, headers=headers)
print(response.json())
```

■ **Benefit:** Reduces manual task entry and ensures issues are tracked in ClickUp.

2️⃣ Integrating ClickUp with External Databases

Teams that use external project tracking tools, CRMs, or data warehouses can sync data with ClickUp using the API.

📌 Example – Syncing ClickUp Tasks with Google Sheets Using Python:

```python
import gspread
from oauth2client.service_account import ServiceAccountCredentials
import requests

# Authenticate Google Sheets API
scope = ["https://spreadsheets.google.com/feeds",
"https://www.googleapis.com/auth/drive"]
creds = ServiceAccountCredentials.from_json_keyfile_name("credentials.json", scope)
client = gspread.authorize(creds)

# Open the Google Sheet
sheet = client.open("ClickUp Task Tracker").sheet1

# Fetch tasks from ClickUp API
api_key = "YOUR_API_KEY"
list_id = "123456789"
url = f"https://api.clickup.com/api/v2/list/{list_id}/task"
headers = {"Authorization": api_key, "Content-Type": "application/json"}

response = requests.get(url, headers=headers)
```

```
tasks = response.json()["tasks"]

# Update Google Sheet
for idx, task in enumerate(tasks, start=2):
    sheet.update(f"A{idx}", task["name"])
    sheet.update(f"B{idx}", task["status"]["status"])
```

⬛ **Benefit:** Keeps external reports updated automatically.

---

③ Generating Custom Reports Using ClickUp API

ClickUp's API can pull real-time project data for advanced analytics in Power BI, Tableau, or custom dashboards.

📌 **Example – Fetching Task Progress Data for a Dashboard:**

```
import requests
import pandas as pd

api_key = "YOUR_API_KEY"
list_id = "123456789"
url = f"https://api.clickup.com/api/v2/list/{list_id}/task"

headers = {"Authorization": api_key, "Content-Type": "application/json"}
response = requests.get(url, headers=headers)
tasks = response.json()["tasks"]

# Convert data to a DataFrame
task_data = [{"Task Name": task["name"], "Status": task["status"]["status"]} for
task in tasks]
df = pd.DataFrame(task_data)

# Display DataFrame
print(df)
```

⬛ **Benefit:** Enables real-time tracking of task completion rates and bottlenecks.

---

④ Automating Notifications & Status Updates

Teams can use the API to automatically notify team members via Slack or email when a ClickUp task reaches a specific status.

📌 **Example – Sending a Slack Message When a Task is Completed:**

```
import requests

slack_webhook_url = "YOUR_SLACK_WEBHOOK_URL"
clickup_api_key = "YOUR_API_KEY"
task_id = "123456789"

# Check task status in ClickUp
task_url = f"https://api.clickup.com/api/v2/task/{task_id}"
headers = {"Authorization": clickup_api_key, "Content-Type": "application/json"}
response = requests.get(task_url, headers=headers)
task_status = response.json()["status"]["status"]
```

```
# Send Slack notification if the task is completed
if task_status.lower() == "completed":
    slack_message = {"text": f"Task '{response.json()['name']}' has been
completed!"}
    requests.post(slack_webhook_url, json=slack_message)
```

■ **Benefit:** Keeps teams informed in real-time without manual follow-ups.

📌 Best Practices for Implementing ClickUp API Solutions

✔1️⃣ **Use Secure API Authentication**
■ Store API keys in **environment variables** instead of hardcoding them in scripts.
■ Use **OAuth2 for enterprise-level security** when available.

✔2️⃣ **Leverage Webhooks for Real-Time Updates**
■ Instead of running scheduled scripts, use **ClickUp Webhooks** to trigger updates automatically.

✔3️⃣ **Optimize API Calls to Avoid Rate Limits**
■ ClickUp's API **limits the number of requests per minute**. Batch requests efficiently to stay within limits.

✔4️⃣ **Test API Calls in a Sandbox Environment**
■ Use **test lists or spaces** to avoid unintended modifications in live projects.

✔5️⃣ **Document API Workflows for Team Collaboration**
■ Keep **detailed API documentation** to help team members understand and maintain custom integrations.

🚀 Final Thoughts: Enhancing ClickUp with API Customization

By leveraging **ClickUp's API**, teams can:
■ **Automate repetitive workflows** to improve efficiency.
■ **Sync external databases and tools for seamless collaboration.**
■ **Extract and visualize ClickUp data for better decision-making.**
■ **Enable real-time notifications and status tracking.**

In the next chapter, we'll explore **how to use ClickUp browser extensions for quick task capture and workflow efficiency.**

Browser Extensions for Quick Task Capture

In a fast-paced work environment, capturing tasks efficiently is **crucial for productivity**. Often, team members come across tasks while browsing emails, researching, or managing customer support—yet manually adding them to ClickUp **takes extra time** and can lead to **missed action items**.

With the **ClickUp Browser Extension**, users can:

◼ **Quickly capture tasks from any webpage**
◼ **Save and annotate screenshots directly into ClickUp**
◼ **Track time spent on tasks without switching tabs**
◼ **Turn emails into ClickUp tasks seamlessly**

Without using the extension, teams may struggle with:

✘ **Forgetting important action items while working in a browser**
✘ **Copy-pasting content manually into ClickUp**
✘ **Switching between multiple tools to manage tasks**
✘ **Losing productivity due to inefficient task tracking**

In this chapter, we'll explore:
◼ **How to install and set up the ClickUp browser extension**
◼ **Key features for task capture and productivity**
◼ **Use cases for different teams and workflows**
◼ **Best practices for maximizing efficiency**

📌 How to Install and Set Up the ClickUp Browser Extension

The ClickUp Browser Extension is available for:
✔ **Google Chrome**
✔ **Mozilla Firefox**
✔ **Microsoft Edge**

1 Installing the ClickUp Browser Extension

1 Open your browser and go to the **Chrome Web Store** (or equivalent for other browsers).
2 Search for **ClickUp Browser Extension**.
3 Click **"Add to Chrome" (or Install for your browser)**.
4 Once installed, click on the **ClickUp icon** in the toolbar.
5 Log in with your ClickUp credentials and select a workspace.

📌 Example – Installing the Extension in Chrome:
◼ Open Chrome → Go to the [Chrome Web Store] (https://chrome.google.com/webstore/) → Search for "ClickUp" → Click **"Add to Chrome"** → Done!

💡 Best Practice: Pin the ClickUp extension to your browser toolbar for quick access.

📌 Key Features of the ClickUp Browser Extension

Once installed, the extension provides several **powerful task management features**:

✔ **Quick Task Creation** – Add new tasks directly from the browser.
✔ **Website Bookmarking** – Save web pages into ClickUp tasks for reference.

✔ **Screenshots & Annotations** – Capture images of web content and mark them up.
✔ **Time Tracking** – Monitor time spent on tasks without switching tools.
✔ **Email to Task Conversion** – Turn Gmail messages into actionable ClickUp tasks.

Let's explore each feature in more detail.

---

②Quick Task Creation from Any Webpage

The browser extension allows users to **create tasks instantly** without opening ClickUp.

How to Create a Task from a Webpage

☐ Click the **ClickUp icon** in your browser toolbar.
② Select **"Create New Task"**.
③ Choose a **workspace, list, and status**.
④ Add a **title, description, due date, and priority**.
⑤ Click **"Add Task"** – it's instantly saved to ClickUp!

📌 **Example – A Content Writer Capturing Blog Ideas:**
■ While researching, they find a great article.
■ They open the ClickUp extension, create a task titled "Blog Inspiration."
■ They add a link to the article and assign the task to themselves.

💡 **Best Practice: Use task templates to speed up task creation for recurring workflows.**

---

③Bookmarking Web Pages for Future Reference

The ClickUp extension lets users **save articles, reports, or research material** directly into ClickUp tasks.

How to Save a Webpage to ClickUp

☐ Open the ClickUp extension.
② Click **"Save Page as Task"**.
③ Choose the ClickUp **workspace and list**.
④ Add **notes** or a **due date**.
⑤ Click **"Add Task"** – the page is now saved for later!

📌 **Example – A Product Manager Tracking Market Trends:**
■ They come across a competitor's feature announcement.
■ They save the webpage to ClickUp under "Market Research."
■ The team later reviews it to adapt their strategy.

💡 **Best Practice: Use a dedicated ClickUp list for saved articles and resources.**

---

④Capturing Screenshots & Annotating Directly in ClickUp

With the **screenshot tool**, users can **capture and edit** images before adding them to a task.

How to Take and Annotate Screenshots

☐ Open the ClickUp extension.
② Select **"Capture Screenshot"** (Full Page or Selected Area).

③ Use **markup tools** to highlight important details.
④ Save the image to a ClickUp task with **notes and due dates**.

📌 **Example – A QA Tester Reporting Website Bugs:**
■ They find a broken button on a webpage.
■ They take a screenshot and annotate the issue.
■ They save it as a ClickUp task for the development team.

💡 **Best Practice: Use screenshots to provide context instead of writing long descriptions.**

---

⑤ Tracking Time Without Leaving Your Browser

The ClickUp extension includes a **time tracker** that records how long users work on tasks.

How to Track Time Using the ClickUp Extension

① Open a task in ClickUp.
② Click the **"Start Timer"** button in the extension.
③ Work on the task while the timer runs.
④ Click **"Stop Timer"** when finished.

📌 **Example – A Freelancer Logging Billable Hours:**
■ They start the timer when working on a design project.
■ The total time is logged in ClickUp for accurate invoicing.

💡 **Best Practice: Use time tracking reports in ClickUp to analyze productivity trends.**

---

⑥ Turning Emails into ClickUp Tasks

With Gmail integration, users can convert **important emails** into ClickUp tasks.

How to Convert an Email into a ClickUp Task

① Open Gmail and select an email.
② Click the ClickUp **"Add Task"** button in Gmail.
③ Choose the **workspace, assignee, and priority**.
④ Click **"Save to ClickUp"** – the email is now a task!

📌 **Example – A Sales Team Managing Client Inquiries:**
■ A client sends a request via email.
■ The sales team converts it into a ClickUp task with a due date.
■ The team follows up directly from ClickUp.

💡 **Best Practice: Use task comments to discuss email tasks with teammates instead of forwarding emails.**

📌 Best Practices for Maximizing Efficiency with ClickUp Browser Extensions

✔① **Use the Extension for Quick Idea Capture**
■ Whenever you come across an **important task or article**, save it immediately to ClickUp.

✔② **Reduce Manual Data Entry with Screenshots & Annotations**
■ Instead of typing long explanations, use **annotated screenshots** to communicate visually.

✔ 3 Track Time for Productivity Insights
■ Use the **time tracker** to monitor how long tasks take and optimize workflows.

✔ 4 Convert Emails to Tasks for Seamless Communication
■ Instead of copying information manually, **turn emails into actionable ClickUp tasks**.

✔ 5 Customize Notifications to Avoid Overload
■ Set up **personalized ClickUp notifications** to stay informed without distractions.

🚀 Final Thoughts: Boosting Productivity with ClickUp Browser Extensions

By using the ClickUp Browser Extension, teams can:
■ **Capture tasks instantly without switching apps**
■ **Store research and articles directly in ClickUp**
■ **Save time by using screenshots instead of lengthy explanations**
■ **Log work hours effortlessly with time tracking**
■ **Turn important emails into actionable tasks**

In the next chapter, we'll explore **real-world case studies of teams using ClickUp for complex projects.**

Section 7:
Case Studies and Real-World Examples

Tech Startup: Managing Agile Sprints in ClickUp

Tech startups operate in **fast-paced environments** where product development, customer feedback, and business objectives are constantly evolving. Without an **agile project management framework**, startups may face:

✘ Delayed product releases due to inefficient workflows
✘ Lack of prioritization, leading to scope creep
✘ Poor collaboration between development, design, and marketing teams
✘ Inconsistent tracking of progress, leading to missed deadlines

By using **ClickUp to manage Agile sprints**, startups can:

■ Structure development cycles efficiently using Agile principles
■ Ensure transparent and streamlined task assignments
■ Track sprint progress using Kanban boards, Gantt charts, and dashboards
■ Leverage automation to reduce manual work in sprint planning

In this case study, we'll explore:
■ How a tech startup structured Agile sprints in ClickUp
■ Key ClickUp features that enhanced sprint execution
■ Best practices for iterative development and backlog management
■ How the startup improved efficiency using ClickUp automation

---

📌 Agile Sprint Structure in ClickUp

Company Overview:
A tech startup, **CodeFlow**, develops AI-powered project management tools. Their development team follows **two-week Agile sprints** to implement new features, resolve bugs, and optimize the product based on user feedback.

Challenges Before ClickUp:
- **Lack of centralized sprint tracking** → Tasks were scattered across multiple tools.
- **Inefficient backlog prioritization** → No clear roadmap for upcoming features.
- **Limited visibility into sprint progress** → No real-time insights into bottlenecks.

1️⃣ Setting Up Sprint Workflows in ClickUp

The **CodeFlow team structured their Agile workflow** in ClickUp using:

✔ **Spaces** → One dedicated space for software development.
✔ **Folders** → Separate folders for **Backlog, Current Sprint, and Completed Sprints**.
✔ **Lists** → Feature Development, Bug Fixes, Testing & QA.
✔ **Custom Statuses** → "Backlog → In Progress → Review → Testing → Done."

📌 **Example – ClickUp Structure for Sprint Workflows:**

- Software Development (Space)
  - ├── 📁 Sprint Backlog (Folder)
  - │   ├── ■ Feature Development (List)
  - │   ├── 🐞 Bug Fixes (List)
  - │   ├── 🔥 Testing & QA (List)
  - ├── 📁 Current Sprint (Folder)
  - ├── 📁 Completed Sprints (Folder)

💡 **Best Practice: Use Spaces for high-level organization, Folders for sprint cycles, and Lists for task categories.**

📌 Sprint Planning in ClickUp

②Managing the Product Backlog

The backlog contains **all upcoming feature requests, bug fixes, and technical improvements**. Before each sprint, the team:

✔ **Prioritizes tasks using ClickUp Custom Fields** (e.g., High, Medium, Low priority).
✔ **Estimates effort using Story Points in Custom Fields**.
✔ **Uses ClickUp Docs to document feature specifications.**

📌 **Example – Prioritizing Tasks for a New Feature:**
■ **Feature:** "AI-based Task Recommendations"
■ **Priority:** High
■ **Estimated Effort:** 8 Story Points
■ **Assigned Sprint:** Sprint 15

💡 **Best Practice: Use the Priority Custom Field and Story Points to estimate effort before adding tasks to a sprint.**

---

③Creating Sprint Boards with ClickUp Views

ClickUp offers multiple views to **visualize sprint progress efficiently**.

- **Kanban Board View** – Organizes sprint tasks based on statuses.
- **List View** – Displays all sprint tasks in one place.
- **Gantt Chart View** – Tracks dependencies and sprint timelines.
- **Calendar View** – Helps teams align development schedules with deadlines.

📌 **Example – Using ClickUp Views for Sprint Execution:**
■ **Sprint Planning:** Use the List View to filter tasks assigned to the current sprint.
■ **Sprint Execution:** Developers use the Kanban Board to track daily progress.
■ **Sprint Review:** The Gantt Chart provides an overview of completed vs. pending work.

💡 **Best Practice: Use Board View for daily standups and List View for backlog grooming.**

---

④Automating Repetitive Sprint Tasks

To reduce **manual work**, the CodeFlow team leveraged **ClickUp Automations** for:

✔ **Automatic Sprint Start & End Notifications**
✔ **Task Assignments Based on Sprint Selection**
✔ **Recurring Tasks for Retrospectives & Sprint Reviews**

📌 **Example – Automating Task Assignments:**
■ **Trigger:** When a task is moved to "Sprint 16," assign it to the Sprint Lead.
■ **Action:** Automatically change status to "In Progress."

💡 **Best Practice: Automate repetitive workflows like sprint planning and task movement.**

📌 Sprint Execution & Tracking in ClickUp

5 Tracking Sprint Progress with Dashboards

To monitor sprint success, the team used ClickUp **Dashboards** with:

✔ **Task Progress Chart** – Visualizing tasks completed vs. pending.
✔ **Velocity Chart** – Tracking average work completed per sprint.
✔ **Burndown Chart** – Measuring how quickly sprint tasks are completed.

📌 **Example – Sprint Dashboard Widgets:**
■ **Completed vs. Pending Tasks Chart** – Displays task completion rates.
■ **Sprint Velocity Report** – Helps predict future sprint capacity.
■ **Bug Resolution Tracker** – Tracks resolved vs. new bug reports.

💡 **Best Practice: Use ClickUp Dashboards to visualize sprint progress in real-time.**

---

6 Running Sprint Reviews & Retrospectives

At the end of each sprint, the CodeFlow team:

✔ **Held a Sprint Review using ClickUp Docs** to document feedback.
✔ **Used Custom Statuses to mark completed vs. incomplete tasks.**
✔ **Added retrospective action items as new tasks for improvement.**

📌 **Example – A Sprint Retrospective in ClickUp Docs:**

What Went Well	What Could Be Improved	Action Items
Faster bug resolution	More clarity in feature requirements	Standardize feature request documentation
Good collaboration	Need to improve test case coverage	Add QA checklist to each feature task

💡 **Best Practice: Use ClickUp Docs to document sprint learnings and improvements.**

📌 Key Outcomes of Using ClickUp for Agile Sprints

By implementing ClickUp for Agile sprint management, **CodeFlow achieved:**

■ **30% faster sprint execution** due to streamlined workflows.
■ **Reduced manual work** using Automations for sprint planning.
■ **Improved collaboration** across teams with integrated Docs, Comments, and Chat.
■ **Enhanced transparency** using Dashboards for real-time progress tracking.

🚀 **Final Thoughts: How Startups Can Use ClickUp for Agile Sprints**

Tech startups can **maximize development efficiency** using ClickUp by:
■ **Creating structured Spaces for backlog, sprints, and completed work**
■ **Using Kanban Boards, Gantt Charts, and Dashboards for progress tracking**
■ **Leveraging Automations to reduce repetitive sprint management tasks**
■ **Conducting structured Sprint Reviews and Retrospectives in ClickUp Docs**

In the next case study, we'll explore how a **marketing agency uses ClickUp to manage multi-client campaigns.**

Marketing Agency: Multi-Client Campaign Coordination

Marketing agencies handle **multiple clients, simultaneous campaigns, and tight deadlines**, requiring seamless collaboration and efficient task management. Without a structured workflow, agencies face:

✗ **Missed deadlines due to poor task tracking**
✗ **Difficulty managing multiple campaigns simultaneously**
✗ **Lack of transparency in client approvals and feedback loops**
✗ **Scattered assets, making it hard to find the latest content versions**

By using **ClickUp for multi-client campaign coordination**, agencies can:

■ **Centralize campaign planning in one platform**
■ **Improve task visibility and team accountability**
■ **Streamline content approvals and client communication**
■ **Automate repetitive tasks to save time**

In this case study, we'll explore how a **digital marketing agency structured its ClickUp workspace** to handle multiple client campaigns efficiently.

📌 Structuring ClickUp for Multi-Client Campaigns

Agency Overview:
A digital marketing agency, **BrandMaven**, manages **15+ clients** across industries, each requiring different marketing strategies, deliverables, and timelines.

Challenges Before ClickUp:
- **No centralized campaign tracking** – Tasks and assets were scattered across emails, spreadsheets, and chat apps.
- **Client feedback was disorganized** – Difficult to track revisions and approvals.
- **Time-consuming reporting** – No automated way to track campaign performance.

1️⃣ Setting Up a Multi-Client Workspace in ClickUp

BrandMaven structured their ClickUp workspace to ensure **clear separation between client projects while keeping everything accessible**.

✔ **Spaces** → One dedicated space for each client.
✔ **Folders** → Separate folders for each campaign (e.g., Social Media, Email, PPC).
✔ **Lists** → Lists for content creation, approvals, and analytics.
✔ **Custom Statuses** → "Planned → In Progress → Review → Approved → Published."

📌 Example – ClickUp Structure for Multi-Client Management:

- Marketing Agency Workspace
  - 📁 Client A (Space)
    - ■ Social Media Campaigns (Folder)
    - ■ Email Marketing (Folder)
    - ■ PPC Ads (Folder)
  - 📁 Client B (Space)
  - 📁 Client C (Space)
  - 📁 Internal Operations (Folder)

📍 **Best Practice: Use Spaces for each client, Folders for different campaign types, and Lists for detailed task tracking.**

📌 Planning & Executing Marketing Campaigns in ClickUp

2️⃣ Managing Campaign Timelines with Gantt Charts

BrandMaven used ClickUp's **Gantt Chart View** to map out **content calendars, email campaigns, and ad schedules**.

📌 **How They Used Gantt Charts:**
⬛ **Mapped campaign timelines** to ensure deliverables met deadlines.
⬛ **Linked dependent tasks** (e.g., "Ad Design" must be completed before "Campaign Launch").
⬛ **Tracked overlapping deadlines** across multiple clients to prevent scheduling conflicts.

📍 **Best Practice: Use ClickUp's Dependency feature to ensure content creation and approval stages follow a logical flow.**

3️⃣ Organizing Content Production with Board View

BrandMaven used **ClickUp's Kanban Board View** for tracking:

✔ **Blog articles** – Topic research → Drafting → Editing → Publishing.
✔ **Social media posts** – Graphics → Copywriting → Client approval → Scheduling.
✔ **Paid ads** – Creative design → A/B testing → Launch.

📌 **Example – Social Media Campaign Workflow:**

Task	Status
Create Instagram post for Product X	In Progress
Write Facebook ad copy for Client A	Review
Schedule Twitter posts for next week	Approved

📍 **Best Practice: Use Custom Fields to categorize content by platform (Instagram, LinkedIn, TikTok, etc.).**

4️⃣ Streamlining Client Approvals with ClickUp Docs & Comments

A major challenge for BrandMaven was **managing client feedback**. Before ClickUp, clients **sent approvals via email**, making it hard to track changes.

📌 **How ClickUp Simplified Approvals:**
⬛ **ClickUp Docs for content drafts** → Clients reviewed and commented directly.
⬛ **Task Comments for quick feedback** → Eliminated long email threads.
⬛ **Custom Status: "Waiting for Approval"** → Tracked pending approvals in one place.

📍 **Best Practice: Tag clients in ClickUp comments instead of sending emails to reduce communication delays.**

📌 Using ClickUp Automations for Marketing Workflow Efficiency

5 Automating Repetitive Tasks

To **save time on manual work**, BrandMaven automated:

✔ **Content scheduling** → When a post is marked "Approved," it moves to "Scheduled."
✔ **Client follow-ups** → If a task is in "Review" for more than 3 days, ClickUp sends a reminder.
✔ **Recurring reporting** → Automated generation of weekly campaign performance reports.

📌 **Example – Automation for Client Reminders:**
■ **Trigger:** If a task is in "Waiting for Approval" for **3+ days** → Notify the client via ClickUp.
■ **Action:** Change task priority to "Urgent" if no response after 5 days.

💡 Best Practice: Use Automations to send reminders and reduce delays in campaign execution.

📌 Tracking Campaign Performance with ClickUp Dashboards

6 Creating Custom Dashboards for Real-Time Insights

To track **campaign performance**, BrandMaven used **ClickUp Dashboards** with:

✔ **Engagement Metrics** – Social media interactions and click-through rates.
✔ **Ad Spend vs. ROI Reports** – PPC performance data.
✔ **Content Status Reports** – Overview of completed vs. pending tasks.

📌 **Example – Weekly Client Dashboard Metrics:**

Metric	Performance
Facebook Ad CTR	5.2% (↑ 0.8%)
Instagram Engagement Rate	8.5% (↑ 1.2%)
Blog Article Read Time	3 min (↓ 10s)

💡 Best Practice: Share dashboards with clients for transparent, real-time campaign tracking.

📌 Key Outcomes of Using ClickUp for Multi-Client Campaigns

By implementing ClickUp, **BrandMaven achieved:**

■ **40% faster campaign execution** due to streamlined workflows.
■ **Improved collaboration** between teams and clients.
■ **Better content tracking** with ClickUp Docs and Board View.
■ **Automated approval reminders**, reducing client follow-up delays.

🏹 Final Thoughts: How Agencies Can Optimize Campaign Coordination with ClickUp

Marketing agencies can **maximize efficiency** in ClickUp by:

■ Creating separate Spaces for each client to keep campaigns organized
■ Using Gantt Charts and Board Views to manage deadlines and task statuses
■ Leveraging Automations to reduce manual follow-ups and speed up approvals
■ Implementing ClickUp Dashboards for real-time performance tracking

In the next case study, we'll explore how **healthcare organizations use ClickUp for compliance and task tracking.**

Healthcare Project: Compliance and Task Tracking

Healthcare organizations operate in a **highly regulated environment**, where **compliance with industry standards, patient safety, and operational efficiency** are critical. Managing healthcare projects often involves:

■ **Ensuring compliance with HIPAA, GDPR, or other regulatory requirements**
■ **Coordinating tasks across multiple departments (clinicians, IT, administrators, etc.)**
■ **Tracking medical procedures, patient workflows, and documentation**
■ **Managing complex approval processes for policy updates and audits**

Without a **structured project management system**, healthcare teams may struggle with:

✗ **Missed deadlines for compliance audits and reporting**
✗ **Inefficient tracking of operational improvements**
✗ **Lack of real-time visibility into task status and responsibilities**
✗ **Data security risks due to fragmented documentation**

In this case study, we'll explore how **a hospital network leveraged ClickUp** to improve compliance tracking, project execution, and team coordination.

📌 Structuring ClickUp for Healthcare Compliance & Task Management

1️⃣ The Challenge: Managing Compliance and Internal Projects

Organization Overview:
A regional **hospital network** with multiple facilities needed a system to:

✔ Track **compliance audits and policy updates**
✔ Improve **collaboration between medical, IT, and administrative teams**
✔ Reduce **manual tracking of patient workflow improvements**
✔ Ensure **timely completion of operational improvement projects**

Challenges Before ClickUp:
 • **Disorganized documentation** – Compliance documents scattered across emails and shared drives.
 • **Lack of visibility into task progress** – No central location for compliance deadlines and projects.
 • **Manual compliance tracking** – Teams used spreadsheets, leading to errors and inefficiencies.

2️⃣ Creating a ClickUp Workspace for Compliance & Operations

The hospital structured its ClickUp workspace to **separate compliance, task tracking, and operational projects** while ensuring clear **team responsibilities**.

📌 ClickUp Structure for Healthcare Compliance & Projects:

 • Healthcare Compliance & Operations (Workspace)
   ├── 🚩 Regulatory Compliance (Folder)
   │   ├── ■ HIPAA Compliance Audits (List)
   │   ├── ■ GDPR Data Security Checks (List)
   │   ├── ■ Policy Updates & Approvals (List)
   ├── 🚩 Operational Improvements (Folder)
   │   ├── 🔧 Patient Workflow Enhancements (List)
   │   ├── ■ Hospital Equipment Maintenance (List)

| ├── ■ Staff Training & Certifications (List)

💡 **Best Practice: Use Spaces for different functional areas, Folders for compliance categories, and Lists for specific tasks.**

📌 Tracking Compliance Tasks in ClickUp

③ Managing Compliance Audits with Custom Statuses & Checklists

The hospital's compliance team used ClickUp to track **regulatory audits** across multiple locations.

✔ **Custom Statuses** – "Not Started → In Progress → Under Review → Approved → Completed"
✔ **Task Templates for Repetitive Compliance Checks**
✔ **Checklists for Required Documents (e.g., HIPAA security policies, GDPR assessments, etc.)**

📌 **Example – HIPAA Compliance Audit Checklist in ClickUp:**

■ Security risk assessment completed
■ Employee HIPAA training documented
■ Access logs reviewed for compliance
■ Policy updates approved by compliance team

💡 **Best Practice: Use ClickUp Checklists to standardize compliance procedures and prevent missing steps.**

---

④ Automating Recurring Compliance Tasks

To **prevent missed deadlines**, the hospital set up **ClickUp Automations** for:

✔ **Recurring compliance audits** every **quarter**
✔ **Automatic notifications** for policy reviews **every six months**
✔ **Escalation reminders** if tasks remained in "Under Review" for more than a week

📌 **Example – Automating Compliance Task Reminders:**
■ **Trigger:** If an audit checklist remains incomplete for 5 days, **send an alert to the compliance officer**.
■ **Action:** Change task priority to **Urgent** and assign to the compliance manager.

💡 **Best Practice: Automate compliance tracking to ensure no deadlines are missed.**

📌 Managing Healthcare Operations in ClickUp

⑤ Coordinating Patient Workflow Improvements

To improve **patient flow in emergency rooms**, the hospital:

✔ Created a **Task List for patient triage improvements**
✔ Used **Dependencies** to ensure tasks followed a logical sequence (e.g., "Review patient intake process" must be completed before "Update triage protocol")
✔ Used the **Gantt Chart View** to monitor progress and identify bottlenecks

📌 **Example – ClickUp Workflow for Patient Flow Enhancements:**

Task	Assigned To	Status
Review current intake process	Operations Team	In Progress
Identify bottlenecks in triage	ER Head	Pending
Implement new triage protocol	Chief Medical Officer	Not Started

💡 **Best Practice: Use Gantt Charts to track process improvement initiatives across multiple teams.**

---

6 Tracking Equipment Maintenance & Staff Training

The hospital **tracked medical equipment maintenance** and **staff training certifications** in ClickUp.

✔ **Equipment Maintenance:**
■ Used **ClickUp Docs** to store maintenance logs.
■ Set up **recurring maintenance tasks** for MRI machines, ventilators, and other critical equipment.

✔ **Staff Training & Certifications:**
■ Used **Custom Fields** to track certification expiration dates.
■ Automated **reminders for upcoming renewals** (e.g., CPR training, HIPAA certification).

📌 **Example – ClickUp Dashboard for Training & Equipment Maintenance:**

Task	Due Date	Status
MRI Machine Maintenance	April 15	Scheduled
HIPAA Training for New Staff	May 1	In Progress
CPR Certification Renewal	June 10	Pending

💡 **Best Practice: Use ClickUp Reminders to alert staff about upcoming training renewals and equipment maintenance deadlines.**

📌 Key Outcomes of Using ClickUp for Healthcare Compliance & Operations

By implementing ClickUp, the hospital achieved:

■ **25% reduction in compliance audit errors** due to structured task tracking.
■ **Improved team collaboration** with real-time updates on regulatory changes.
■ **Automated reminders and escalations** reduced missed deadlines by 40%.
■ **Better visibility into operational projects**, leading to **faster process improvements**.

🚀 Final Thoughts: How Healthcare Organizations Can Use ClickUp for Compliance & Operations

Healthcare teams can **maximize efficiency** in ClickUp by:

■ **Structuring Spaces, Folders, and Lists for compliance tracking and operational workflows**
■ **Using Custom Statuses and Checklists to ensure audits and policy reviews are thorough**

■ Automating recurring compliance tasks and staff training reminders
■ Leveraging Dashboards to track key performance metrics in real-time

In the next case study, we'll explore **how remote teams use ClickUp for global workflow synchronization.**

Remote Team: Global Workflow Synchronization

Remote teams operate across **different time zones, locations, and cultural work styles**, making efficient collaboration **crucial** for productivity. Without a structured system, teams often struggle with:

✗ **Lack of visibility into task progress and deadlines**
✗ **Inefficient communication leading to delays**
✗ **Difficulty in tracking time-sensitive projects across time zones**
✗ **Disorganized document and file management**

ClickUp enables remote teams to **synchronize workflows globally** by providing:

▪ **A centralized workspace for project planning, task tracking, and documentation**
▪ **Asynchronous collaboration tools for teams working in different time zones**
▪ **Integrated communication features like Comments, Chat, and Docs**
▪ **Automation for scheduling, reporting, and reminders to eliminate manual work**

In this case study, we'll explore how a **fully remote software development team** used ClickUp to overcome workflow challenges and improve productivity.

📌 Structuring ClickUp for a Remote Global Team

1️⃣ The Challenge: Managing Work Across Time Zones

Company Overview:
A remote-first SaaS company, **CloudSync Solutions**, has a development team **spread across North America, Europe, and Asia**. Their key challenges included:

- **Delayed responses due to time zone differences**
- **Task status ambiguity—team members unsure who was responsible for what**
- **Difficulty tracking project progress across different departments**
- **Lack of centralized documentation and asynchronous updates**

2️⃣ Creating a Remote-Friendly ClickUp Workspace

To enhance **global workflow synchronization**, CloudSync Solutions structured their ClickUp workspace as follows:

📌 ClickUp Structure for a Remote Team:

- Remote Team Workspace
  - 📁 Product Development (Folder)
    - ▪ Sprint Planning (List)
    - ▪ Feature Requests (List)
    - 🐞 Bug Tracking (List)
  - 📁 Operations (Folder)
    - 🏋 Onboarding & Training (List)
    - 💬 Team Communication & Meetings (List)
    - 📕 Documentation & Knowledge Base (Docs)
  - 📁 Marketing & Sales (Folder)
    - 📣 Campaign Planning (List)
    - ▪ Performance Metrics (Dashboard)

📍 **Best Practice: Use ClickUp Spaces for different departments, Folders for major projects, and Lists for task tracking.**

📌 **Task Management & Collaboration in ClickUp**

3️⃣ **Assigning Clear Responsibilities with Custom Statuses & Assignees**

To avoid confusion, ClickUp tasks included:

✔ **Custom Statuses** – "To Do → In Progress → Waiting for Review → Done"
✔ **Multiple Assignees for Cross-Team Work** – A developer and a tester on the same task
✔ **Task Dependencies** – "Bug Fix A" must be completed before "Feature Release B"

📌 **Example – Task Ownership for a Feature Development Sprint:**

Task	Assigned To	Status
Develop API for payment gateway	Dev Team	In Progress
Conduct security testing for API	QA Team	Waiting for Review
Deploy API to production	DevOps	Not Started

📍 **Best Practice: Use ClickUp's Custom Statuses and Dependencies to clarify task ownership.**

4️⃣ **Managing Asynchronous Communication with ClickUp Docs & Comments**

With teams working across time zones, **real-time meetings weren't always possible**. Instead, CloudSync Solutions used:

✔ **ClickUp Docs** for asynchronous updates on product changes and project status.
✔ **Task Comments** for detailed discussions instead of long email threads.
✔ **Threaded Chat & @mentions** to keep team members engaged and informed.

📌 **Example – ClickUp Docs for Asynchronous Standups:**

Date	Team Member	Update
March 12	Alice (US)	Completed API integration, waiting for QA feedback.
March 13	Raj (India)	QA test cases updated, ready for execution.
March 14	Marco (Spain)	Reviewing API test results and deploying fixes.

📍 **Best Practice: Use ClickUp Docs to document daily standups asynchronously, allowing team members in different time zones to update progress at their convenience.**

📌 **Automating Workflows for Efficiency**

⑤ Automating Task Assignments and Reminders

To keep work moving smoothly, CloudSync Solutions **automated**:

✔ **Recurring Standup Updates** – ClickUp auto-creates a "Daily Update" task for each team member.
✔ **Task Reassignments** – Once a developer marks a task as "Done," it automatically assigns to QA.
✔ **Deadline Reminders** – If a task is overdue by **two days**, ClickUp sends a reminder.

📌 **Example – ClickUp Automation for a Development Sprint:**

⬛ **Trigger:** When a developer marks a task as **"Completed"** →
⬛ **Action:** Automatically assign it to **QA for testing** and change status to **"Waiting for Review"**.

💡 **Best Practice: Use ClickUp Automations to reduce manual follow-ups and speed up task transitions.**

📌 Tracking Team Performance with Dashboards

⑥ Creating Dashboards for Real-Time Global Insights

To track **team productivity and project health**, CloudSync Solutions built **custom ClickUp Dashboards** with:

✔ **Task Completion Rates** – Progress bars for each department.
✔ **Time Tracking Reports** – Logged hours per task and team member.
✔ **Sprint Burndown Chart** – Monitoring remaining work vs. sprint completion.

📌 **Example – ClickUp Dashboard Metrics:**

Metric	Performance
Sprint Completion %	85% (↑ 5%)
Average Task Completion Time	2.5 days (↓ 0.3 days)
Overdue Tasks	2 (↓ 3 tasks)

💡 **Best Practice: Use ClickUp Dashboards to get real-time insights into remote team performance.**

📌 Key Outcomes of Using ClickUp for Global Workflow Synchronization

By using ClickUp, CloudSync Solutions achieved:

⬛ **30% faster project turnaround time** due to clearer task assignments.
⬛ **More efficient asynchronous communication**, reducing unnecessary meetings.
⬛ **Automated workflows**, minimizing time spent on repetitive task management.
⬛ **Improved team alignment**, ensuring global teams stayed on the same page.

🏁 Final Thoughts: How Remote Teams Can Use ClickUp for Global Collaboration

Remote teams can **optimize their workflows** in ClickUp by:

- Structuring Spaces, Folders, and Lists for global task management
- Using Docs and Comments for asynchronous updates instead of relying on meetings
- Automating task assignments, standups, and reminders to reduce manual work
- Leveraging Dashboards to track real-time team performance across time zones

In the next section, we'll explore **how to troubleshoot common ClickUp errors and optimize performance** for complex projects.

Section 8:
Troubleshooting and Optimization

Common Errors and How to Resolve Them

While ClickUp is a powerful tool for managing complex projects, **users often encounter issues that hinder productivity**. These errors range from **misconfigured settings, workflow inefficiencies, performance lags, and data loss concerns**. This chapter covers the **most common errors users face in ClickUp** and provides **step-by-step solutions** to resolve them efficiently.

📌1 Task and Status Mismanagement

Issue: Tasks Stuck in the Wrong Status or Missing from Views

Users often **misplace tasks** due to:
* Incorrect **custom statuses**
* Filters hiding certain tasks
* Tasks **not properly assigned** to Lists

Solution

■ **Check Task Filters:** Ensure that your view filters (e.g., "Only Show Open Tasks") are not hiding tasks.
■ **Review Task Statuses:** If a task isn't moving forward, verify that it follows your project's workflow.
■ **Use Automations:** Set up **automatic status changes** when conditions are met (e.g., when a subtask is completed, move the parent task forward).
■ **Use ClickUp's "Everything View"** to **search for missing tasks across all projects**.

📌 **Best Practice:** Create **clear, standardized workflows** with well-defined **custom statuses** to prevent bottlenecks.

📌2 Notifications Overload or Missing Alerts

Issue: Too Many or Too Few Notifications

Many users complain that they **receive excessive notifications**, while others miss critical alerts.

Solution

■ **Customize Notification Settings:**

* Go to **ClickUp Settings > Notifications** and fine-tune what you receive.
* Disable irrelevant updates like "Someone viewed this task."

■ **Use ClickUp's Notification Center** to clear and filter alerts based on importance.

■ **For Missed Notifications:**

* Ensure you're **watching tasks** you need updates on.

- Enable **email notifications** for key actions.

📌 **Best Practice: Encourage teams to use task comments instead of direct notifications** for non-urgent discussions.

📌 3 Slow Performance and Lag Issues

Issue: ClickUp Freezing or Loading Slowly

ClickUp's performance **can degrade due to**:
- Too many **open tasks and views**
- Large numbers of **custom fields and attachments**
- Browser extensions interfering with ClickUp

Solution

■ **Clear Browser Cache:** ClickUp relies on **browser storage**—clearing your cache improves performance.
■ **Use ClickUp's Desktop App** instead of the web version for **better stability**.
■ **Reduce Open Views:** Avoid keeping too many views open at once—optimize by using **Dashboards** instead.
■ **Disable Heavy Automations:** Complex automations may slow ClickUp down—**simplify redundant ones**.

📌 **Best Practice:** Regularly **archive old projects and clear completed tasks** to keep ClickUp running smoothly.

📌 4 Issues with ClickUp Automations

Issue: Automations Not Running as Expected

ClickUp Automations **fail due to**:
- **Conflicting rules** (e.g., automation loops)
- Tasks not **matching trigger conditions**
- **Overlapping automation steps**

Solution

■ **Check Automation Logs:** ClickUp provides logs under **Automations > History** to debug failed workflows.
■ **Test Automations on a Sample Task** before rolling them out team-wide.
■ **Avoid Overlapping Triggers:** For example, don't create an automation that **moves a task while another automation changes its status**—this causes conflicts.

📌 **Best Practice: Use fewer, more effective automations** instead of creating unnecessary ones.

📌 5 ClickUp Integrations Not Syncing Properly

Issue: ClickUp Not Syncing with Google Drive, Slack, or Other Apps

ClickUp integrations **sometimes fail** due to:
- **Expired permissions**

- Sync conflicts with other tools
- API limitations

Solution

■ **Reauthorize the Integration:** Disconnect and reconnect the app under **Settings > Integrations**.
■ **Check Permission Levels:** Ensure you **have admin-level access** to integrate ClickUp with external tools.
■ **Use Webhooks or ClickUp API** for advanced integration troubleshooting.

📌 **Best Practice: Periodically check all integrations** and refresh them if necessary.

📌 6 Recurring Tasks Not Functioning Correctly

Issue: Recurring Tasks Not Duplicating or Resetting Properly

Users report that **recurring tasks** sometimes:
- Don't **repeat on schedule**
- Overwrite **previous instances**
- Create duplicates unexpectedly

Solution

■ **Set the Correct Recurrence Type:** Choose between

- **Recurring by Due Date** (task resets but keeps past history)
- **Recurring by Completion** (creates a new task when the old one is done)

■ **Use Task Templates for Recurring Workflows:** If tasks need the same subtasks and checklists, **use templates** instead of duplicating manually.

📌 **Best Practice: Test recurrence settings** before applying them to critical workflows.

📌 7 Task Dependencies and Subtasks Not Functioning Correctly

Issue: Dependencies Not Enforcing Task Order

ClickUp allows you to **set dependencies** (e.g., Task B starts only when Task A is completed), but sometimes:
- Tasks **don't block correctly**
- Dependencies **don't trigger automations**
- Team members **work on blocked tasks by mistake**

Solution

■ **Enable Dependency Enforcement:** In ClickUp settings, turn on **"Prevent Starting Blocked Tasks"** to **enforce** workflow order.
■ **Use "Waiting On" or "Blocking" Links:** Instead of simple relationships, use **ClickUp's dependency features** for better tracking.
■ **Visualize Dependencies with Gantt Charts:** ClickUp's Gantt view highlights **task dependencies** with clear flow lines.

📌 **Best Practice: Educate your team on using dependencies properly** to maintain structured workflows.

📌8 ClickUp Time Tracking Not Logging Correctly

Issue: Missing or Incorrect Time Logs

Users report **ClickUp's time tracking doesn't always register work correctly**, causing discrepancies in reports.

Solution

■ **Check Time Tracking Settings:** Ensure time logging is enabled in **Workspace Settings**.
■ **Manually Adjust Logs:** Use ClickUp's **Time Log View** to edit incorrect entries.
■ **Use Third-Party Integrations:** If ClickUp's built-in tracking is unreliable, use **Toggl or Harvest** for better accuracy.

📌 **Best Practice: Regularly audit time logs** to ensure accuracy before generating reports.

Final Thoughts: How to Troubleshoot ClickUp Like a Pro

ClickUp is a robust platform, but **errors can slow down your workflow**. The key to **quick troubleshooting** is:

■ **Regularly auditing your settings and workflows**
■ **Using ClickUp's Automation and Notification Logs for debugging**
■ **Leveraging ClickUp's support forums and knowledge base** for solutions
■ **Optimizing performance by keeping ClickUp clean and organized**

By proactively **resolving common issues**, you can ensure that ClickUp remains a **highly efficient project management tool** for your team.

Optimizing ClickUp for Speed and Performance

ClickUp is a **powerful, feature-rich project management tool**, but as workspaces grow in complexity, performance issues can arise. **Slow loading times, lagging tasks, and inefficient workflows** can reduce productivity.

This chapter provides **proven strategies** to optimize ClickUp for **speed and efficiency**, ensuring a **seamless user experience** even when managing **large, complex projects**.

📌1 Minimizing ClickUp Lag & Improving Load Speeds

Issue: ClickUp Running Slowly or Freezing

ClickUp may slow down due to:
* **Overloaded workspaces** with too many active tasks and views
* **High resource usage from custom fields, automations, and dependencies**
* **Heavy storage usage due to large attachments**

Solution

■ **Reduce Open Views & Tabs:**

* Avoid keeping **multiple ClickUp tabs open at once**—this consumes memory.
* Instead, use **Dashboards** for centralized tracking.

■ **Archive or Close Completed Tasks & Lists:**

* **Old projects and tasks slow down ClickUp** if left open.
* Use **Task Automations** to **automatically archive** completed work.

■ **Limit Unused Custom Fields:**

* Too many custom fields per task **increase load times**.
* Regularly **audit** and **delete unnecessary fields**.

■ **Reduce Attachments & Use External Storage:**

* Large files in ClickUp **slow down performance**.
* Store documents in **Google Drive, Dropbox, or OneDrive** instead of directly in ClickUp.

📌 **Best Practice:** Keep ClickUp **lean** by **archiving outdated tasks, limiting custom fields, and reducing attachment sizes**.

📌2 Optimizing ClickUp Views & Dashboards

Issue: Slow-Loading Views & Laggy Dashboards

Views that display **hundreds of tasks** or rely on **complex filters and formulas** can load slowly.

Solution

■ **Use Filters & Smart Views:**

* Instead of **displaying all tasks**, apply **filters** to only show:

- ○ Open or active tasks
- ○ High-priority items
- ○ Tasks due within the next 30 days

Limit Dashboard Widgets:

- **Too many widgets** on a Dashboard **slow down loading times**.
- Keep dashboards **focused on essential metrics**.

Favor List View Over Board View for Large Projects:

- **Board views require more processing power**—use **List View** for speed.
- Split **large project boards** into smaller categories.

📌 **Best Practice:** Keep views **simple and targeted**—**avoid overloading dashboards** with excessive widgets and data.

📌3 Optimizing ClickUp Automations for Efficiency

Issue: Automations Running Slowly or Failing

Complex workflows **with multiple automations** can:
- ◆ Cause **delays in task updates**
- ◆ **Trigger unintended loops**, slowing ClickUp down
- ◆ **Overwhelm system resources**, making ClickUp lag

Solution

Audit & Remove Redundant Automations:

- Too many triggers can **slow down task execution**.
- Combine **similar automations** instead of creating multiple separate ones.

Limit Automations to Critical Actions:

- Use **only essential automations** (e.g., changing task status, sending alerts).
- Avoid unnecessary actions like **"change task priority if a comment is added"**—this can **trigger excessive updates**.

Test Automations on Small Sample Tasks:

- Before applying automations **across large projects**, test them in a **sandbox workspace**.

📌 **Best Practice:** Use **fewer, smarter automations** to **keep workflows smooth** and **reduce processing time**.

📌4 Browser & App Optimizations for Speed

Issue: ClickUp Running Slowly on Web Browsers

The ClickUp **web app** relies on browser resources—performance **can suffer** if:
- ◆ Too many browser extensions are enabled
- ◆ The browser cache is full
- ◆ The internet connection is slow

Solution

■ **Use ClickUp's Desktop App:**

- The **desktop version** often runs faster than the web app.

■ **Disable Unnecessary Browser Extensions:**

- Some **ad blockers and security extensions** interfere with ClickUp's functionality.

■ **Clear Browser Cache & Cookies Regularly:**

- **Chrome & Edge:** `Settings > Privacy > Clear browsing data`
- **Firefox:** `Options > Privacy & Security > Clear Data`

■ **Check Internet Speed & Connection Stability:**

- Slow internet can cause **ClickUp lag**—use a wired connection for better stability.

📌 **Best Practice:** Use ClickUp's **desktop app or a lightweight browser** with **minimal extensions** for **faster performance**.

📌 5 Managing ClickUp Workspaces for Maximum Efficiency

Issue: Cluttered Workspaces with Too Many Tasks & Lists

A **disorganized ClickUp workspace** leads to:
- ◆ Difficulty finding important tasks
- ◆ Slower search results
- ◆ Longer task load times

Solution

■ **Organize Tasks with Nested Folders & Lists:**

- Use **Folders** to group similar projects instead of **long, cluttered Lists**.
- Example:

- ◆ Product Development (Folder)
  ├── ■ Sprints (List)
  ├── 🛠 Bug Fixes (List)
  ├── ■ Feature Requests (List)

■ **Use Tags & Custom Fields Wisely:**

- Instead of **dozens of Lists**, use **Tags** and **Custom Fields** to categorize tasks.

■ **Regularly Archive Old Projects & Unused Tasks:**

- ClickUp slows down when storing **too much old data**—archive or delete old projects.

📌 **Best Practice:** Keep ClickUp **clean and structured**—use **Folders, Tags, and Custom Fields** effectively.

📌 6 Using ClickUp's Performance Mode & Settings Adjustments

Issue: Slow Loading Speed for Large Workspaces

ClickUp provides **performance settings** that help speed up workspaces.

Solution

■ **Enable Performance Mode:**

- Go to `ClickUp Settings > Preferences` and enable **Performance Mode** to **reduce animations and speed up navigation**.

■ **Disable Unused Features:**

- If your team doesn't use **Time Tracking, Chat, or Docs**, disable them under **Workspace Settings**.

■ **Optimize ClickUp Mobile App for Speed:**

- Disable **background sync** in mobile settings if ClickUp is **draining battery or running slow**.

📌 **Best Practice:** Enable **Performance Mode** and **disable unused features** to streamline ClickUp's responsiveness.

Final Thoughts: Keeping ClickUp Fast & Efficient

To **maximize performance**, teams should:

■ **Archive old tasks, reduce custom fields, and use external storage for attachments**
■ **Optimize ClickUp views & dashboards to reduce loading times**
■ **Limit automations and ensure they don't overlap**
■ **Use ClickUp's desktop app for faster performance**
■ **Enable Performance Mode & disable unnecessary features**

By following these best practices, ClickUp will **run faster, load efficiently, and remain scalable** for complex project management.

Staying Updated with New Features and Tools

ClickUp is constantly evolving, introducing **new features, integrations, and optimizations** to enhance productivity. However, staying updated with these changes is **essential** to ensure your workflows remain efficient and leverage the **latest advancements**.

This chapter provides a **strategic approach** to staying informed about ClickUp updates, evaluating new tools, and implementing them into your **complex project management workflows** without disruption.

📌1 Where to Find ClickUp Updates

ClickUp regularly **releases new features, bug fixes, and improvements**, but many users **miss these updates**. To stay ahead, consider the following sources:

⬛ ClickUp Release Notes

- ClickUp publishes all feature updates in their **Release Notes section**:
    - 📍 [ClickUp's Latest Release Notes] (https://clickup.com/release-notes)
- This page provides details on **new functionalities, bug fixes, and enhancements**.

⬛ ClickUp Blog & Newsletter

- The ClickUp blog offers **in-depth guides, feature breakdowns, and use-case examples**.
- Sign up for the **ClickUp newsletter** to receive updates directly in your inbox.

⬛ ClickUp Community & Forums

- Engage with other users and ClickUp experts in:
    - 📍 [ClickUp Community Forum] (https://community.clickup.com/)
    - 📍 [ClickUp Facebook Groups] (https://www.facebook.com/groups/ClickUpCommunity)

⬛ Follow ClickUp on Social Media

- **Twitter (X), LinkedIn, and YouTube** often feature **product updates, feature demos, and webinars**.
    - ○ [ClickUp on Twitter] (https://twitter.com/clickup)
    - ○ [ClickUp on LinkedIn]n(https://www.linkedin.com/company/clickup/)
    - ○ [ClickUp's YouTube Channel] (https://www.youtube.com/c/ClickUpApp)

📌 **Best Practice:** Bookmark **ClickUp's Release Notes** and subscribe to the **newsletter** for instant updates.

📌2 How to Test & Evaluate New Features

Issue: New Features Can Disrupt Workflows If Implemented Without Testing

While new features are exciting, **immediate implementation can lead to workflow disruptions**. Before rolling them out, follow a **structured evaluation process**:

Solution

⬛ Use ClickUp's Demo Workspace

- Set up a **testing workspace** in ClickUp to trial new features **without affecting active projects**.

■ **Read the Feature Documentation**

- Before enabling a new feature, review ClickUp's **official guides and FAQs**.

■ **Train Team Members Before Enabling New Features**

- Conduct a **quick internal session or create a ClickUp Doc** explaining the feature's benefits and use cases.

■ **Test Feature Impact on Automations and Dependencies**

- Some updates **affect existing automations, integrations, or dependencies—test before activating**.

📌 **Best Practice: Test updates in a controlled environment before implementing them company-wide**.

📌3 Leveraging ClickUp's Newest Features for Efficiency

Here are some of ClickUp's **most powerful recent updates** and how they **enhance complex project management**:

■ **ClickUp AI for Task Automation & Writing**

What it does:

- AI-powered suggestions for **task descriptions, summaries, and brainstorming**.
- Automates **report generation, emails, and process documentation**.

How to use it effectively:
✔ Use ClickUp AI to generate **meeting summaries, task breakdowns, and action items**.
✔ Automate **daily standups and progress reports** with AI-generated text.

■ **Whiteboards for Visual Collaboration**

What it does:

- Lets teams **brainstorm, plan workflows, and create flowcharts** visually.
- Integrates directly into **tasks, docs, and dashboards**.

How to use it effectively:
✔ Use Whiteboards for **project roadmaps and dependency mapping**.
✔ Create **visual mind maps** for brainstorming before breaking down tasks.

■ **Universal Search 2.0 (Advanced Search & Filtering)**

What it does:

- Finds **tasks, docs, comments, and files instantly**, even across **multiple workspaces**.
- Filters results by **assignees, custom fields, and task status**.

How to use it effectively:
✔ Use Universal Search to **track down old project files** without manually browsing lists.
✔ Create **saved search queries** for frequent searches (e.g., "All overdue tasks").

📌 **Best Practice:** Regularly **review and adopt new ClickUp features** that **align with your workflows**.

📌4 Keeping ClickUp Integrations Updated

Many organizations **integrate ClickUp with Slack, Google Drive, Zoom, and other tools**—but **integrations need maintenance** to remain effective.

Issue: Outdated Integrations Can Cause Sync Errors & Lost Data

Solution

■ **Reauthorize Integrations Regularly**

- Some integrations **expire or lose permissions** over time.
- Check **Settings > Integrations** and refresh authorizations **every few months**.

■ **Monitor Integration Logs**

- ClickUp provides logs for API integrations—check these for **sync errors**.

■ **Test New Integration Features**

- ClickUp **frequently updates integrations,** such as **new Slack commands or Google Drive enhancements**.

📌 **Best Practice: Periodically review integrations** to ensure **data flows smoothly between ClickUp and external tools**.

📌5 Participating in ClickUp Beta Testing for Early Access

For those who want **early access to new tools,** ClickUp's **Beta Program** offers a chance to **test new features before they are publicly released**.

How to Join ClickUp Beta Testing

■ Visit **ClickUp's Beta Signup Page**: [ClickUp Beta Program] (https://clickup.com/beta)
■ Enable **Beta Features in Settings**
■ Provide **feedback to ClickUp's team** for improvements

📌 **Best Practice:** If your team relies on **stability,** avoid enabling **beta features on critical workspaces**—test them separately first.

📌6 Keeping Your Team Trained on ClickUp's Updates

Issue: Teams Struggle to Adapt to New Features Without Training

If your team is unaware of **new functionalities,** they may **miss out on productivity boosts** or **become frustrated with interface changes**.

Solution

■ **Host Monthly ClickUp Training Sessions**

- Dedicate **30 minutes per month** to introduce **new features and best practices**.

■ **Create ClickUp Docs for Internal SOPs**

- Maintain an **updated document** outlining **feature changes and team guidelines**.

■ **Assign a ClickUp Admin or Power User**

- Have a **team champion** responsible for **evaluating, testing, and rolling out** new features.

📌 **Best Practice: Keep your team informed and trained** on ClickUp's evolving toolset to maximize adoption.

Final Thoughts: How to Stay Ahead in ClickUp

ClickUp is **continuously evolving**, and **staying informed** ensures your team **remains productive and efficient**.

To stay updated:
■ **Subscribe to ClickUp's Release Notes & Blog**
■ **Test new features in a sandbox workspace before applying them**
■ **Reauthorize and update integrations to prevent sync issues**
■ **Use ClickUp Beta Testing for early access to innovations**
■ **Train your team regularly to maximize new tools**

By adopting these strategies, your organization will **leverage the best of ClickUp's evolving capabilities**, keeping your **complex project management workflows optimized and future-ready**.

Section 9:
The Future and Final Tips

The Future of ClickUp in Project Management

As **technology and work environments evolve**, project management tools must **adapt to new challenges, automation, and team structures**. ClickUp has positioned itself as a **leading project management platform**, continuously **expanding its features and integrations** to support **agile, remote, and complex workflows**.

This chapter explores the **future of ClickUp in project management**, highlighting **emerging trends, upcoming features, AI-driven improvements, and its role in enterprise growth**.

📌1 The Rise of AI & Automation in ClickUp

The Role of AI in Project Management

The **future of ClickUp** is closely tied to **artificial intelligence (AI)** and **machine learning (ML)**, which will enhance how teams **plan, execute, and optimize projects**.

Upcoming AI-Driven Enhancements in ClickUp

- **Automated Task Creation & Suggestions**

  - AI will recommend **subtasks, dependencies, and deadlines** based on historical data.

- **AI-Powered Smart Summaries**

  - ClickUp AI will generate **meeting notes, progress reports, and status updates automatically**.

- **Predictive Risk Analysis**

  - AI will analyze **project timelines** and warn about **potential delays before they happen**.

- **Smart Task Prioritization**

  - AI will assess workload and **suggest task priorities dynamically** based on **urgency, dependencies, and workload distribution**.

📌 Future Impact: AI will **reduce manual workload, prevent project bottlenecks, and help teams make data-driven decisions faster**.

📌2 ClickUp's Expansion into Enterprise-Level Project Management

Why Enterprises are Adopting ClickUp

As large organizations **transition from traditional tools** (like MS Project, Asana, and Jira) to ClickUp, the platform is evolving to meet **enterprise demands**:

■ Scalability & Performance Enhancements

- Future updates will **increase ClickUp's speed and stability**, even for **teams managing 100,000+ tasks**.

■ Improved Enterprise Security & Compliance

- More **data encryption, SOC 2 compliance, and user permission controls** will make ClickUp a top choice for **regulated industries** like **finance and healthcare**.

■ Enterprise-Level Resource Management

- ClickUp will introduce **more advanced workforce allocation tools**, allowing **HR, finance, and project teams** to track resources effectively.

📌 **Future Impact:** ClickUp will evolve into a **leading enterprise project management tool**, rivaling **Jira, ServiceNow, and Microsoft Project**.

📌3 Seamless Cross-Platform Integrations & API Advancements

ClickUp's Future Integrations & API Upgrades

- **Deeper Integration with AI Assistants (ChatGPT, Google Bard, Microsoft Copilot)**

  - Teams will be able to **ask AI-powered chatbots for project updates, reports, and analytics within ClickUp**.

- **Expanded No-Code & Low-Code Automation**

  - ClickUp's API will allow teams to **build fully customized workflows without advanced programming skills**.

- **Advanced BI & Data Analytics Integrations**

  - Expect **seamless integrations with Power BI, Tableau, and Google Data Studio** for **real-time analytics on team performance, revenue impact, and efficiency**.

📌 **Future Impact:** ClickUp will become a **fully integrated hub**, eliminating the need for **multiple disconnected apps**.

📌4 The Evolution of Remote Work & ClickUp's Role

ClickUp as the Ultimate Remote Work Platform

The **future of work is remote**, and ClickUp is adapting to **support distributed teams** with:

■ Enhanced Asynchronous Communication Features

- ClickUp will likely **expand voice notes, video updates, and AI-generated summaries** for better remote collaboration.

■ Global Time Zone Adjustments

- Task scheduling and deadlines will automatically **adjust based on each user's time zone**.

■ Built-In Virtual Whiteboards & Team Collaboration Tools

- Expect **advanced brainstorming whiteboards and live collaboration modes** for teams working across different locations.

📌 **Future Impact:** ClickUp will **redefine remote project management** by eliminating **time zone barriers and communication gaps**.

📌5 Customization & Industry-Specific ClickUp Solutions

Industry-Specific ClickUp Workspaces

ClickUp will move toward **customized templates and features** for different industries, including:

- **Software Development → Agile sprint planning & DevOps integrations**
- **Marketing Teams → Campaign tracking & social media automation**
- **Healthcare & Compliance → HIPAA-compliant project management**
- **Manufacturing & Supply Chain → Real-time tracking & logistics tools**

📌 **Future Impact:** ClickUp will become a **more industry-tailored platform**, providing **pre-built workflows for different sectors**.

📌6 The Future of ClickUp's User Experience & UI

ClickUp is **constantly refining its interface** to improve **speed, usability, and navigation**. Upcoming UI changes include:

■ A More Intuitive ClickUp 3.0 Interface

- Faster, cleaner, and **less cluttered dashboard layouts**.

■ Customizable AI-Powered Dashboards

- ClickUp will offer **automated data insights** that suggest **real-time project optimizations**.

■ Improved Mobile App Experience

- Expect a **redesigned mobile app** with **faster task entry, voice commands, and real-time notifications**.

📌 **Future Impact:** ClickUp will deliver a **simplified, AI-enhanced user experience**, making **complex project management more accessible**.

📌7 Predictions: Where ClickUp is Headed by 2030

By 2030, ClickUp is expected to:

✔ **Compete directly with Microsoft Project and Jira as the #1 enterprise project management tool.**
✔ **Become an AI-driven platform**, automating **task prioritization, reporting, and resource allocation**.
✔ **Expand into specialized industries**, offering **custom solutions for finance, healthcare, and construction**.
✔ **Introduce virtual reality (VR) project management spaces** for **immersive collaboration**.
✔ **Eliminate reliance on third-party apps**, consolidating **all productivity tools into ClickUp**.

📌 **Final Thought:** ClickUp is **not just a project management tool**—it's evolving into an **intelligent work management ecosystem**.

Final Thoughts: Preparing for ClickUp's Future

To **stay ahead of the curve**, organizations should:

■ **Regularly monitor ClickUp's roadmap & beta test new features**.
■ **Embrace AI-powered automation to streamline workflows**.
■ **Use integrations to connect ClickUp with analytics and business intelligence tools**.
■ **Train teams to leverage ClickUp's evolving features for maximum efficiency**.

ClickUp's future is **bright, innovative, and AI-driven**—adapting to these advancements will **position your team for long-term success** in project management.

Final Tips for Sustaining Productivity Gains

Adopting ClickUp for **complex project management** is a **major step toward increased productivity**, but **long-term success** depends on **maintaining efficiency** and **adapting to evolving workflows**.

This final chapter provides **practical strategies** to ensure that your **team, processes, and tools** continue to **deliver maximum efficiency and productivity gains** over time.

📌1 Continuously Optimize Workflows

Issue: Stagnant Workflows Lead to Productivity Decline

Once teams establish their **ClickUp structure**, it's easy to **fall into routine patterns**—but **periodic optimization is crucial** for continued efficiency.

Solution: Perform Regular Workflow Audits

■ **Quarterly Review of Project Structures**

- Assess **Spaces, Folders, and Lists** to ensure they align with **current business needs**.
- Archive **inactive projects** and refine **task hierarchies** for clarity.

■ **Optimize Task Templates & Automation**

- Identify **manual processes** that can be **automated using ClickUp Automations**.
- Update **task templates** to reflect **evolving project needs**.

■ **Refine Task Prioritization & Custom Fields**

- Review **Custom Fields** to remove **unnecessary data points**.
- Adjust **priorities, dependencies, and statuses** based on team feedback.

📌 **Best Practice: Set a recurring ClickUp task for quarterly workflow audits** to eliminate inefficiencies.

📌2 Promote a Culture of Accountability & Transparency

Issue: Lack of Accountability Can Cause Delays & Bottlenecks

Without clear ownership, teams **struggle to track progress**, leading to **missed deadlines** and **communication breakdowns**.

Solution: Establish Strong Accountability Practices

■ **Use ClickUp's Assigned Comments & Mentions**

- Tag team members in **comments and task descriptions** to assign ownership.

■ **Leverage Workload View to Balance Team Capacity**

- Monitor team availability and **redistribute tasks** to prevent **overburdening key individuals**.

■ **Set Up Weekly Progress Reports & Dashboards**

- Create **custom dashboards** that highlight:
  - **Task completion rates**
  - **Project delays & blockers**
  - **Team workload & efficiency**

📌 Best Practice: Encourage transparency by making project dashboards accessible to all stakeholders.

📌3️⃣ Train & Upskill Your Team on ClickUp Best Practices

Issue: Underutilization of ClickUp's Features Leads to Wasted Potential

Many teams **use only a fraction of ClickUp's capabilities**, missing out on **productivity-enhancing features**.

Solution: Ongoing ClickUp Training & Adoption Programs

⬛ **Host Monthly ClickUp Training Sessions**

- Cover **new features, automation strategies, and best practices**.

⬛ **Encourage Team Members to Take ClickUp University Courses**
📍 [ClickUp University] (https://university.clickup.com) provides **free training on advanced workflows, automations, and integrations**.

⬛ **Nominate ClickUp Power Users in Each Department**

- Appoint **one or two team members** to **test new features** and share **best practices with colleagues**.

📌 Best Practice: Encourage ClickUp certification among key project managers to **maximize platform efficiency**.

📌4️⃣ Automate Repetitive Tasks for Maximum Efficiency

Issue: Manual Work Consumes Time That Could Be Spent on Strategy

Teams often waste hours **performing repetitive actions**, such as **updating task statuses or sending follow-ups**.

Solution: Implement ClickUp Automations

⬛ **Automate Task Assignments & Due Dates**

- Use **Triggers & Actions** to **auto-assign** tasks when certain conditions are met.

⬛ **Automate Status Updates**

- Set up **rules** to mark tasks as **"In Progress"** when someone **adds a comment or attaches a file**.

⬛ **Integrate with Slack & Email for Auto-Notifications**

- Ensure team members receive **real-time alerts** on important task updates.

📌 **Best Practice: Review automation logs every month** to refine workflows and **remove redundant triggers**.

📌5 **Encourage Asynchronous Collaboration to Reduce Meeting Fatigue**

Issue: Too Many Meetings Reduce Productive Work Time

In complex projects, **frequent meetings disrupt deep work** and **slow down execution**.

Solution: Shift to Asynchronous Workflows in ClickUp

⬛ **Use ClickUp Docs & Whiteboards for Planning**

- Instead of lengthy discussions, **document ideas, updates, and feedback** in ClickUp Docs.

⬛ **Enable Video & Audio Comments for Quick Updates**

- ClickUp's **video recording feature** allows users to **record explanations instead of scheduling unnecessary meetings**.

⬛ **Use ClickUp's Chat & Mentions Instead of Email**

- Consolidate **project-related discussions within ClickUp**, reducing **email overload**.

📌 **Best Practice: Adopt a "meetings-optional" policy by using ClickUp for async collaboration.**

📌6 **Stay Updated on ClickUp's Latest Features**

Issue: Using Outdated Methods Leads to Inefficiency

ClickUp is constantly improving—**not staying up-to-date means missing out on time-saving enhancements**.

Solution: Subscribe to ClickUp Updates & Beta Features

⬛ **Follow ClickUp's Release Notes**
📍 [ClickUp's Release Notes] (https://clickup.com/release-notes) provide **monthly updates** on **new features and improvements**.

⬛ **Join ClickUp's Beta Program**

- Test **early feature releases** before they go public and **adapt workflows in advance**.

⬛ **Follow ClickUp on Social Media & Community Forums**
📍 [ClickUp Community] (https://community.clickup.com/) is a great place to **learn from other power users**.

📌 **Best Practice: Dedicate 30 minutes monthly to exploring new ClickUp updates & implementing relevant features.**

📌7 **Measure & Analyze Productivity Trends Over Time**

Issue: Without Tracking Productivity, Teams Can't Improve

If you don't **track project performance**, it's difficult to identify **bottlenecks and improvement areas**.

Solution: Use ClickUp's Dashboards for Real-Time Insights

■ **Create KPI-Focused Dashboards**

- Monitor key metrics such as:
  - ♦ **Task completion rate**
  - ♦ **Missed vs. met deadlines**
  - ♦ **Team workload distribution**

■ **Use Time Tracking Data to Optimize Resource Allocation**

- Analyze **how much time is spent on tasks** to **identify inefficiencies**.

■ **Conduct Monthly Retrospectives**

- Hold a **quick 30-minute review** to discuss:
  - ✔ What worked well
  - ✔ What didn't
  - ✔ What needs improvement

📌 Best Practice: Use ClickUp's Goals feature to track progress on high-priority initiatives.

Final Thoughts: Sustaining Long-Term Productivity in ClickUp

Adopting ClickUp is **just the first step**—maintaining **high efficiency and productivity gains requires continuous effort**.

To **sustain long-term success**, focus on:

■ **Quarterly workflow audits & optimization**
■ **Training team members on best practices**
■ **Automating repetitive tasks to save time**
■ **Shifting to asynchronous collaboration for fewer meetings**
■ **Staying updated on ClickUp's latest features**
■ **Tracking team performance & refining processes regularly**

By implementing these **strategic approaches**, your organization will not only **maintain productivity gains** but **continue evolving with ClickUp's advancements**.

🚀 **Congratulations on mastering ClickUp for Complex Projects!** ⬤

Appendices

Appendix A: Keyboard Shortcuts Cheat Sheet

ClickUp's keyboard shortcuts significantly enhance productivity by allowing users to navigate, create, edit, and manage tasks efficiently without relying on the mouse. This cheat sheet provides an essential list of shortcuts categorized by their functionality.

◆ Global Navigation Shortcuts

Action	Shortcut (Windows & Mac)
Open QuickSwitch (Jump between tasks, lists, spaces)	Ctrl + K (Cmd + K on Mac)
Open Command Center	Ctrl + / (Cmd + / on Mac)
Open Search	F
Open Notifications	N
Open Profile Settings	O

📌 Task Management Shortcuts

Action	Shortcut (Windows & Mac)
Create a new task	T
Open Task Tray	Q
Delete a task	Shift + Delete
Open task details	Enter
Assign a task to yourself	Me in assignee field
Change task status	S
Set task due date	D
Copy task link	Ctrl + Shift + C (Cmd + Shift + C on Mac)
Archive task	Ctrl + Shift + A (Cmd + Shift + A on Mac)

▪ Quick Formatting in Descriptions, Comments, and Docs

Action	Shortcut
Bold	`Ctrl + B` (Cmd + B on Mac)
Italics	`Ctrl + I` (Cmd + I on Mac)
Underline	`Ctrl + U` (Cmd + U on Mac)
Strikethrough	`Ctrl + Shift + X` (Cmd + Shift + X on Mac)
Create Bullet List	* then Space
Create Numbered List	1. then Space
Create Checklist	[ ] then Space
Insert Code Block	``` + Space
Insert Quote Block	> + Space

▪ Calendar & Time Tracking Shortcuts

Action	Shortcut
Start time tracking	T inside task
Stop time tracking	Esc
Open calendar view	C

📁 Views & Navigation

Action	Shortcut
Switch between List, Board, or Calendar views	V
Open My Work	M
Go to Home	H
Go to Inbox	I

🔗 Miscellaneous Shortcuts

Action	Shortcut
Open settings	P

Open Integrations	G
Close window/dialog	Esc
Toggle full-screen mode	F11

🚀 Pro Tips for Boosting Productivity with Shortcuts

1 **Memorize essential shortcuts** – Focus on T (Create Task), `Ctrl + K` (QuickSwitch), and S (Change Task Status).
2 **Customize your shortcuts** – ClickUp allows you to set custom key mappings.
3 **Use automation with shortcuts** – Combine shortcuts with ClickUp Automations for even faster workflows.

By incorporating these shortcuts into your daily routine, you can **speed up workflow execution**, **reduce clicks**, and **enhance overall efficiency** in managing complex projects. 🚀

Appendix B: Template Library for Complex Projects

ClickUp provides a powerful template system that allows teams to standardize workflows, improve efficiency, and maintain consistency across projects. This appendix includes **pre-built** and **customizable templates** for different complex project types, helping you **kickstart your workflows** and optimize project management.

◆ Why Use Templates in ClickUp?

- **Saves Time** – Reduces repetitive setup work.
- **Standardizes Workflows** – Ensures consistency across projects.
- **Enhances Collaboration** – Teams can follow predefined structures for better coordination.
- **Scalability** – Enables seamless project expansion with minimal adjustments.

📌 Pre-Built ClickUp Templates

ClickUp offers several **ready-to-use** templates that you can **import** and customize. Below are some of the most useful ones for complex projects:

Template Name	Best For	Key Features
Project Management	Large, multi-stage projects	Task lists, Gantt charts, milestones
Agile Scrum	Software development, sprints	Kanban boards, backlog, sprint planning
Marketing Campaign	Content, ads, and promotions	Campaign timeline, social media calendar
Product Development	Iterative product creation	Feature tracking, roadmaps
Client Management	Agencies and consultants	Client database, deliverables tracking
Construction Management	Construction & engineering projects	Resource planning, dependencies
Event Planning	Conferences, webinars, meetups	Vendor coordination, logistics, agenda

◆ Customizable Templates for Complex Projects

Beyond ClickUp's default templates, **custom templates** tailored to your organization's needs provide an even greater advantage. Below are some **highly effective templates** for managing complex projects efficiently.

1️⃣ Enterprise Project Management Template

- **Best For:** Large organizations managing multi-department projects.
- **Features:**
  - ○ 📌 **Task Lists** – Organizes deliverables by department.
  - ○ ■ **Custom Statuses** – "Initiated," "In Progress," "Review," "Completed."
  - ○ ■ **Automations** – Auto-assign tasks when dependencies are cleared.
  - ○ ■ **Dashboards** – KPI tracking & real-time insights.

2 IT & Software Development Workflow

- **Best For:** Development teams using Agile or Waterfall methodologies.
- **Features:**
  - ○ 🏗 **Sprint Boards** – Backlog, active sprints, completed tasks.
  - ○ 📌 **Epics & Features** – Custom fields for grouping related tasks.
  - ○ ✈ **Automations** – Moves tasks to "Testing" when development is complete.
  - ○ 🔧 **Bug Tracking** – Logs, priority levels, resolution status.

3 Multi-Client Agency Management Template

- **Best For:** Marketing agencies, design firms, consulting services.
- **Features:**
  - ○ ■ **Client Database** – Stores all client details in one space.
  - ○ ● **Campaign Tracker** – Milestones, deliverables, feedback loops.
  - ○ ■ **Client Reports** – Weekly progress, performance metrics.
  - ○ 🔧 **Automations** – Auto-create reports & notifications for stakeholders.

4 Compliance & Regulatory Tracking Template

- **Best For:** Healthcare, finance, and legal projects.
- **Features:**
  - ○ ■ **Checklist-Based Workflows** – Ensures compliance steps are followed.
  - ○ ■ **Automated Alerts** – Deadline reminders for audits & reports.
  - ○ 🔍 **Document Storage** – Secure repository for compliance documents.
  - ○ 🏷 **Custom Fields** – Risk level, compliance status, approval tracking.

5 Remote Team & Global Collaboration Template

- **Best For:** Distributed teams working across multiple time zones.
- **Features:**
  - ○ ■ **Time Zone Awareness** – Task deadlines adjusted for team locations.
  - ○ ● **Embedded Communication** – Integrated ClickUp Chat for real-time updates.
  - ○ ● **Goal Tracking** – Team & individual performance objectives.
  - ○ ■ **Automations** – Task handoff notifications for different shifts.

🏋 How to Import and Use Templates in ClickUp

1 Go to "Templates" in ClickUp

- Navigate to the **Templates** section in ClickUp's workspace settings.

2 Choose a Template

- Select from **pre-made templates** or **upload your own.**

3 Customize the Structure

- Modify **task lists, priorities, and automation settings** to fit your workflow.

4 Apply to New Projects

- Use the template for **future projects** to maintain consistency.

🚀 Final Tips for Using Templates Efficiently

✔ **Regularly update templates** – Adjust based on team feedback.
✔ **Use automation within templates** – Reduces repetitive work.
✔ **Keep templates scalable** – Ensure they grow with your project needs.
✔ **Document template usage** – Provide guidance for new team members.

By leveraging these ClickUp templates, teams can **streamline project setup, improve collaboration, and boost overall efficiency** for managing complex projects. 🚀

Appendix C: Glossary of ClickUp Terminology

ClickUp is a feature-rich project management platform with a vast array of functionalities, many of which come with specific terminology. This glossary serves as a **quick reference guide** to help users **understand key terms** and **maximize efficiency** when using ClickUp for complex projects.

◆ ClickUp Workspace & Hierarchy Terms

Term	Definition
Workspace	The highest level in ClickUp's hierarchy, where all projects and teams are managed.
Spaces	Subsections within a Workspace, usually divided by department, project type, or team function.
Folders	A way to organize Lists within a Space, useful for grouping similar projects together.
Lists	The lowest level of ClickUp's hierarchy, where specific tasks are created and managed.
Tasks	Actionable work items that contain descriptions, assignees, due dates, and statuses.
Subtasks	Smaller steps within a Task, helping to break down complex workflows.
Checklists	Simple to-do lists inside a Task, often used for repeated processes or QA steps.
Milestones	Key project checkpoints used to track major progress points.
Statuses	The different phases a task moves through, such as "To Do," "In Progress," or "Completed."

◆ Task Management & Productivity Features

Term	Definition
Custom Fields	User-defined data fields added to Tasks for enhanced categorization and tracking.
Recurring Tasks	Automated tasks that repeat on a set schedule, such as daily, weekly, or monthly.
Task Dependencies	Relationship settings that define which tasks must be completed before others can begin.
Priorities	Task importance levels (Low, Normal, High, Urgent) to help teams focus on critical work.

Tags	Labels added to tasks for quick filtering and searchability.
Task Templates	Pre-built task structures that can be reused for repetitive workflows.
Bulk Actions	Feature that allows users to edit, move, or delete multiple tasks simultaneously.
Time Tracking	Built-in feature to log the time spent on a task for better resource management.
Workload View	A visualization of how tasks are distributed across team members.
Sprint Points	Numeric values assigned to tasks in Agile sprints to estimate effort required.

◆ Views & Visualization Tools

Term	Definition
List View	A standard task list format, displaying tasks in rows with details like due dates and assignees.
Board View	A Kanban-style visual workflow where tasks are arranged in columns by status.
Calendar View	A calendar-based layout that shows task due dates, milestones, and scheduled events.
Gantt Chart	A timeline visualization that displays task dependencies, durations, and project progress.
Timeline View	Similar to a Gantt chart but with a more flexible layout for visualizing task sequences.
Table View	A spreadsheet-like interface that allows for detailed task sorting and filtering.
Mind Map View	A brainstorming tool for visually structuring ideas and project tasks.
Docs View	An integrated documentation space where teams can create and collaborate on notes.
Form View	A feature that allows external users to submit tasks via customizable forms.
Custom Dashboards	Personalized reporting tools that display KPIs, charts, and performance insights.

◆ Automation & Collaboration Features

Term	Definition
Automations	Rules that trigger specific actions based on task updates, reducing manual work.
Dependencies	Task relationships that dictate when certain tasks can start or be completed.
ClickUp Chat	A built-in chat function for real-time team discussions within ClickUp.
Comments & Mentions	Notes added to tasks with "@mentions" to notify team members.
Custom Roles & Permissions	User access levels defining what actions each team member can perform.
Notifications	Alerts that inform users about task updates, comments, and mentions.
Goal Tracking	A feature that helps teams align tasks with higher-level objectives.
Teams	Groups of users who can be assigned to tasks collectively.
Time Estimates	Predictions of how long a task will take to complete.
Workload Management	A tool that helps distribute work evenly across team members.

◆ Integrations & API Features

Term	Definition
ClickUp API	A developer-friendly interface that allows for custom integrations and automation.
Integrations	Built-in connections with apps like Slack, Google Drive, Zoom, and GitHub.
Zapier Integration	A no-code automation tool that connects ClickUp with thousands of external apps.
Webhooks	A feature that sends real-time updates from ClickUp to external platforms.
Single Sign-On (SSO)	Secure login authentication for enterprise users.
Two-Factor Authentication (2FA)	Enhanced security feature requiring an extra verification step for logins.

◆ Reporting & Analytics

Term	Definition
Custom Reports	Tailored analytics dashboards for tracking project performance.
Sprint Reports	Data summaries that help Agile teams review sprint progress.
Time Tracking Reports	Logs and analytics of how time is spent on tasks and projects.
Workload Reports	A breakdown of how tasks are distributed among team members.
Goal Reports	Progress tracking for company-wide or department-specific goals.
User Activity Reports	Insights into individual team member contributions and engagement.

Understanding ClickUp's terminology is essential for efficiently managing complex projects. By using this glossary as a **quick reference**, teams can **navigate ClickUp with confidence**, ensuring **smooth collaboration, productivity, and project success.** 🚀

Appendix D: Resources for Continued Learning

ClickUp is a **continuously evolving** project management tool, and staying updated with the latest features, best practices, and advanced workflows is crucial for maximizing efficiency. This appendix provides a **comprehensive list of resources** to help users **expand their knowledge**, stay ahead of updates, and **connect with the ClickUp community.**

📚 Official ClickUp Resources

Resource	Description	Link
ClickUp Help Center	A knowledge base with step-by-step guides, FAQs, and troubleshooting solutions.	[help.clickup.com] (https://help.clickup.com)
ClickUp University	Free online courses and certifications on ClickUp's core and advanced functionalities.	[university.clickup.com] (https://university.clickup.com)
ClickUp Blog	Regular updates on new features, best practices, and productivity tips.	[clickup.com/blog] (https://clickup.com/blog)
ClickUp Release Notes	Detailed information on the latest feature releases and updates.	[clickup.com/release-notes]n(https://clickup.com/release-notes)
ClickUp Template Center	A collection of pre-made project management templates for different industries.	[clickup.com/templates]n(https://clickup.com/templates)
ClickUp API Documentation	A guide for developers looking to integrate ClickUp with external tools.	[clickup.com/api] (https://clickup.com/api)

🎥 Video Tutorials & Webinars

Resource	Description	Link
ClickUp YouTube Channel	Official video tutorials, feature walkthroughs, and ClickUp best practices.	[YouTube - ClickUp] (https://www.youtube.com/c/ClickUp)
Webinar Library	Recorded and live webinars covering new features and advanced workflows.	[clickup.com/webinars] (https://clickup.com/webinars)
Productivity Hacks Series	A series of short videos demonstrating time-saving ClickUp tips.	[YouTube - Productivity Hacks] (https://www.youtube.com/c/ClickUp)

📌 Community & Support

Resource	Description	Link
ClickUp Community Forum	A space where users discuss best practices, share templates, and ask questions.	[community.clickup.com] (https://community.clickup.com)
ClickUp Facebook Group	A community of ClickUp power users sharing insights and answering questions.	[Facebook - ClickUp Community] (https://www.facebook.com/groups/clickupcommunity)
ClickUp Discord Server	A live chat community for ClickUp enthusiasts, including developers and project managers.	[Discord - ClickUp] (https://discord.gg/clickup)
ClickUp Reddit Community	A space for discussions, troubleshooting, and feature requests.	[Reddit - r/ClickUp] (https://www.reddit.com/r/clickup)

📖 Books & Articles on Productivity & Project Management

Resource	Description	Link
Getting Things Done (David Allen)	A foundational book on personal productivity and task management.	[Amazon] (https://www.amazon.com/dp/0143126563)
The Lean Startup (Eric Ries)	A must-read for Agile project management and iterative workflows.	[Amazon] (https://www.amazon.com/dp/0307887898)
Scrum: The Art of Doing Twice the Work in Half the Time (Jeff Sutherland)	A guide to Agile and Scrum methodologies for project efficiency.	[Amazon] (https://www.amazon.com/dp/038534645X)
The ClickUp Blog	Articles on productivity, remote work, and project management strategies.	[clickup.com/blog] (https://clickup.com/blog)

🔗 Useful Third-Party Integrations & Tools

Tool	Purpose	Link
Zapier	Automate workflows between ClickUp and 5,000+ apps.	[zapier.com] (https://zapier.com)
Slack Integration	Get task updates and manage ClickUp from Slack.	[clickup.com/integrations/slack] (https://clickup.com/integrations/slack)

Google Drive Integration	Attach Google Drive files to ClickUp tasks.	[clickup.com/integrations/google-drive] (https://clickup.com/integrations/google-drive)
Toggl Track	Advanced time tracking integrated with ClickUp.	[toggl.com] (https://www.toggl.com)
Make (formerly Integromat)	A no-code automation tool similar to Zapier.	[make.com] (https://www.make.com)

ClickUp is a **powerful and evolving platform** that offers **endless possibilities** for managing complex projects. By leveraging these resources, users can **enhance their expertise**, **stay up to date with the latest features**, and **unlock ClickUp's full potential** for team productivity and project success. 🚀

Conclusion

Managing complex projects requires **a strategic approach, efficient collaboration**, and **powerful tools** that can **adapt to dynamic workflows**. Throughout this book, we've explored **how ClickUp serves as a versatile platform** to enhance **team productivity, project organization, and long-term planning**.

From **structuring workspaces for scalability** to **leveraging automation, tracking progress with custom dashboards**, and **optimizing workflows with integrations**, ClickUp provides **a robust ecosystem** that **empowers teams to streamline processes and achieve project success**.

Key Takeaways

By now, you should have a **clear understanding** of how to:
✔ **Set up ClickUp for complex projects**, ensuring a structured and scalable hierarchy.
✔ **Customize views**, workflows, and automations to match your team's needs.
✔ **Effectively manage tasks, dependencies, and timelines** to improve project efficiency.
✔ **Collaborate seamlessly with teams and stakeholders**, using real-time communication features.
✔ **Leverage integrations, API capabilities, and templates** to extend ClickUp's functionality.
✔ **Troubleshoot common issues** and **optimize ClickUp's performance** for a smoother experience.

The principles, strategies, and case studies provided in this book **offer a roadmap** for maximizing ClickUp's potential in handling **multi-faceted, high-demand projects** across industries.

Sustaining Long-Term Success with ClickUp

ClickUp is **constantly evolving**, with new features and updates **enhancing project management possibilities**. To stay ahead, consider the following best practices:

- **Regularly update your workflows** based on new ClickUp features.
- **Encourage team feedback** to improve productivity and collaboration.
- **Utilize ClickUp's community and learning resources** to refine your expertise.
- **Continuously iterate and optimize processes** for long-term scalability.

By **adopting a growth mindset**, embracing **continuous learning**, and leveraging ClickUp to its fullest, your team can **consistently achieve greater efficiency, improved project outcomes, and sustainable productivity gains**.

Final Thoughts

Whether you're **managing a global remote team, coordinating large-scale projects, or looking to optimize business operations**, ClickUp provides **the flexibility and depth** needed to **navigate complex workflows with confidence**.

With the knowledge from this book, you are now **equipped to harness ClickUp's full potential**—empowering your team, optimizing processes, and driving project success **like never before**.

Thank you for reading, and here's to your continued success with ClickUp!